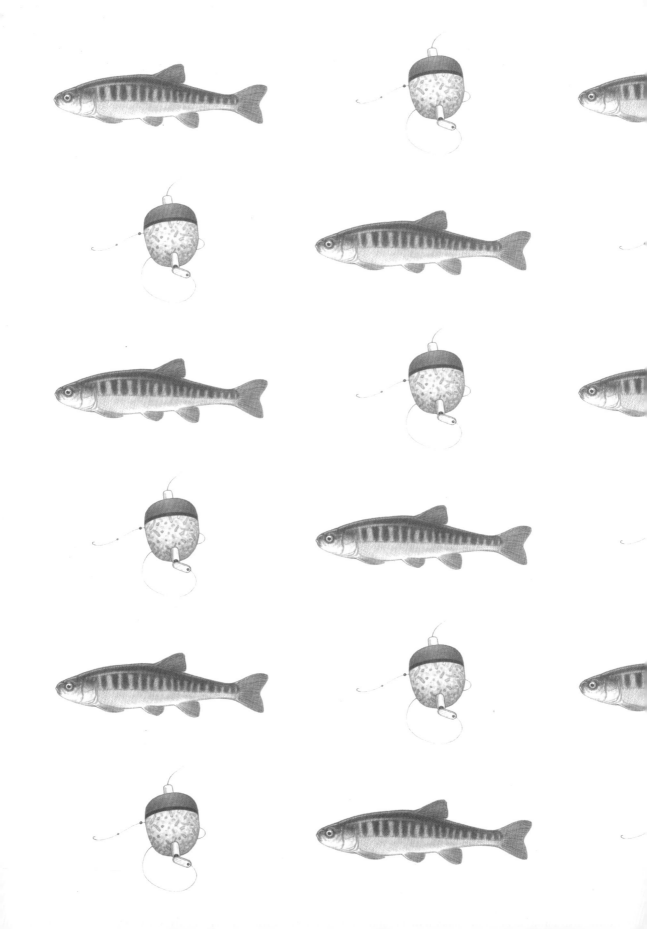

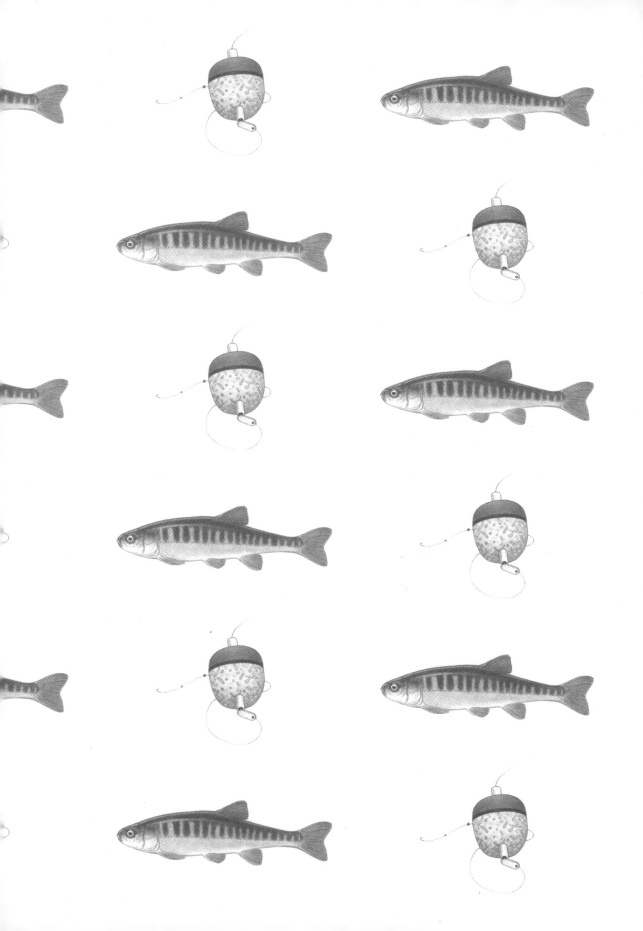

Water Colours

To Steve Collier,
Land's End Inn,

Water Colours
Further ramblings of an artist-angler

Maurice J Pledger

Thank you for a wonderful day,
Maurice J Pledger.

Coch-y-Bonddu Books
2013

Many thanks Steve
Paul Morgan

Thanks for a great day
Lake Edwards

WATER COLOURS
Written and illustrated by Maurice J Pledger

First published by Coch-y-Bonddu Books Ltd, Machynlleth, 2013

Standard edition
High quality paperback with flaps
ISBN 978 1 904784 59 3

Collector's edition
Limited to 250 signed cloth-bound copies
ISBN 978 1 904784 61 6

De luxe leather-bound edition of only 35 copies
ISBN 978 1 904784 62 3

Coch-y-Bonddu Books Ltd, Machynlleth, Powys, SY20 8DG
01654 702837
www.anglebooks.com

To the memory of my Uncle Sergio,
who enriched my childhood and life immeasurably,
and who first inspired me to pick up a brush.

M.J.PLEDGER

ACKNOWLEDGEMENTS

AND SO HERE we are again.

To those of you out across the lake opening these pages for the very first time, I offer my thanks – but as with my first book, *While My Float's Still Cocked,* I can offer you no explanation, nor rhyme nor reason to any of it.

However, to those of you out there who trusted me first time around, I can but hope the meandering path through my memories may unlock for you a few forgotten memories of your own.

The cast of this book remains the same as the first. I make no apologies for this, nor feel the need to. In essence my little group of friends are my most treasured possessions and I cannot but think how blessed I am in having had them share the journey with me. The many memories we've made together are stored in what I call the sixpence jar and, every now and then, I like to take them out, polish them up a little and spread them around. My friends are this book, for in reality the stories and memories herein are just as much a part of their lives as they are mine.

I have only played a supporting role in what is to follow. True, I may be accused of shining my part a little too generously at times while burring theirs a bit too much, but then these are the perks of having the pen.

As before these are nothing more than memories: instances of shared moments which to others might seem insignificant but if, on turning the pages you too find yourself looking back and recalling things which you hold with great affection, then you'll know what this book means to me.

Were it not for Paul Morgan of Coch-y-Bonddu Books my memories would not have found their way to you. His faith and belief in me I can never repay.

And, as before, without the collective magic of my friends Paul Curtis and Pete MacKenzie – my words would have remained on sheets of paper and my paintings on the board. True artists both, thank you so much.

Thanks are also due to Andy, Bob and Rita of Carleton Photographic in Cheshunt for their help in photographing the paintings you see reproduced in the book.

I cannot even begin to thank Basil Ede for the generosity he has shown to me, as long ago as 1966, and again very recently. I suppose in reality he hasn't been aware of the influence his work has had on me throughout my life. Were it not for the incredible beauty of his paintings who knows where my path would have taken me? For those of you not familiar with his work, I would suggest you spend some time reading about him and looking at his paintings. Only then will you realise how fortunate I have been, and how very humbled I am, to read the unbelievably kind words he has written about my own work. Basil, thank you.

So too Bob Roberts: How can I have ever imagined that one day I'd be thanking Bob, someone I've admired from afar for so long, for his very kind words.

The world of fishing is many different things to many different people. The call to leave a warm bed on a dismal winter's night will not be heard by all of us – maybe just one or two. And at the same time, while these hardy souls open the door and trudge off through the snow, others in their beds will be turning over, dreaming of when the warmth of the sun will breathe life back into the stream. And of the little trout which will dimple on the surface just as they did last spring.

A fisher of cod and bass will not begin to feel alive until he stands once again freezing on a deserted storm-lashed beach, while his elderly friend, possibly well into his eighties, will be following his passion just as he did as a child, with an old cane rod resting across his knee waiting for the dabs to bite again. We all have our own tales to tell. Without exception every one of us has memories of this pastime we love.

And these are mine.

If you are looking for a long list of fish or expecting to find top secret baits (I confess there is one and it's not actually mine) and details of implausibly successful methods, I'm afraid you must look elsewhere. (However I do appreciate that there will be some of you whose sparks will be ignited by such matters.)

In my case it just might be the insignificant movement of a lily pad, or seeing the merest notion of a rise by a chub hiding under some trailing alder leaves, that sets my heart racing. Then there are times when an idle thought enters my mind and for a while, often a very long while, my only recourse is to pick up a rod and head off to the river. In particular the forlorn hope of emulating Vince who, many, many, years ago on the River Ouse, caught a little blotchy brown, three-inch burbot. If someone were to ask me which fish in the whole world I would have liked to hold in my hand it would have been that one.

Probably too much to hope for, but we all have our dreams. I'm no different in that respect, but looking back through a world of memories involving my family and closest friends I consider myself rich beyond words.

Should my float dip under tomorrow, I have no complaints.

FOREWORD

I FEEL QUITE sad for people who have never fished. Especially those who tell me it must be boring and ask stupid questions like: 'Do you put maggots in your mouth?' Clearly they lack imagination. I doubt they've ever watched the sun rise over an estate lake on a summer's morning or made friends with a robin on a cold winter's day. Nor could they possibly understand the elastic nature of time when an angler is near water.

Then again, I pity the angler who measures his fishing in pounds and ounces and strives to create an impressive list of PBs, who is obsessed with having the latest rig, the most fashionable bait and can quote the serial numbers of each hook pattern he owns. He also misses the point.

Fishing is not about catching fish, is it? Otherwise we might just as well use seine nets. Or dynamite.

Fishing is about people, places, memories, events, tragedies, hope and elation. It's emotional, and until you understand that, you're not really an angler. You're just someone who happens to go fishing.

The author of this book, Mole to his friends, gets it. He understands. And that's why this book is a delight. It's not a glorified advertorial for some manufacturer's tackle catalogue. It's hardly an eye of toad, wing of bat, alchemistic guide to sure-fire fish catching potions and secret baits either.

It's an insight into an angler's life. It's about people, places and experiences. It's real, and all the better for it. Too many books read like Haynes car manuals. Thankfully this one doesn't.

So what can I say about Mole that really matters? Well, he's a nice man for a start and generous to a fault. When Stuart Walker and I were filming our *Caught in the Act* DVD series we were searching for something unusual

to break up the different 'acts'. 'Wouldn't it be brilliant if we ended each act by fading to a watercolour image of the species we had just fished for?' I suggested.

Stu agreed and so I approached Mole, tentatively, not really expecting him to agree for one moment. Indeed I was shocked when he said, 'I'd be honoured. But let me just run it by Bernard [his agent] first.'

Blow me if he didn't come back really quickly with permission, so we were privileged to include five of Mole's images on each of the four discs and even used his artwork to illustrate the individual disc labels. Boy, do his paintings make our work stand out.

I envy Mole. He breathes life and vibrancy into his fish paintings as you will see in the colour plates. It's a precious gift that makes this book very special and such a pleasant change from the normal smattering of 'sad man holding fish' photographs, particularly the single species works where the same angler is holding up a series of near identical fish, his eyes directed away from the camera towards the fish's head and the inevitably serious facial expression.

I suspect these folk imagine that cracking a smile might in some way diminish the achievement of fooling a cold-blooded creature with a brain the size of a pea. Nothing less than a scowl will do or the invariably long-winded tale of wondrous skill and technical ability required to catch it might not be deemed quite so impressive. It's funny how their success is always by design and never by pure chance. None of these expert fish catchers ever admit to a stroke of good fortune in the way you and I might do.

Fortunately, Mole will never write a book like that. I doubt he could be bothered. No, we should be thankful that we get a different kind of read altogether. I suggest you take this book as a chance to travel back in time, to be enchanted and, moreover, to be entertained. The fish don't have names, nor do you need to acquire a special handshake in order to fish the same waters. So why not sit back and allow your imagination to run riot on an eventful journey that will take you from the fishing tackle shops of Bologna to Redmire via Barclay Park, Hoddeson.

There should be more books like *Water Colours* …

Bob Roberts
2013

EARLY DAYS

To choose a few memories from so many would be as pointless as trying to count the stars.

Bologna

ON THE 21ST of May 1992 news came through from Bologna that my wonderful Uncle Sergio (at the far too early age of 63) had died.

Inconsolable, I took my black American cocker spaniel, Bunny, to the massive field at the Amwell roundabout on the outskirts of Hoddesdon, walked across and, in the middle of nowhere, cried my eyes out.

Then I walked … and walked … until, far from anywhere and at the height of my grief, I was forced to a stop – by a most wonderful, intoxicating, hauntingly familiar, sweet smell which seemed to wrap all around me. When I walked on the smell faded. So I backtracked and again was bathed in the delicious waves. It was Bologna. Without doubt Uncle Sergio was with me. I didn't understand or know what the aroma was, only that I knew things would be okay.

It wasn't until maybe a year later, while walking Bunny again in a small area of parkland near our home that I noticed the air flooded by the same heady aroma and I realised what it was. Following it, I found myself walking over to a row of tall trees – western balsam poplars. The same trees, I immediately recognised, that were part of the sensory background to the many wonderful holidays I had spent in Bologna visiting my mother's family when I was so much younger. Western balsam poplars grew in profusion in the region, especially alongside rivers and lakes. Standing amongst those trees, closing my eyes and breathing deeply, I was whirling in memories of my youth.

From the time I was born until the age of about 20, Mum and I spent six weeks of every summer with my grandmother, 'Nonna' Medea, and my Uncle Athos and Aunty Vera at their home in the old city centre of Bologna, a short ten-minute walk along Via Maggiore from the Due Torri (the two towers), Asinelli and Garisenda. A twenty-minute bus ride across to the outskirts of the city towards Casalecchio, lived my other uncle and aunty, 'Zio' Sergio and 'Zia' Laura. Dad would join us for the last two weeks, when we all holidayed together, either in the Italian Dolomites or somewhere at the seaside along the Adriatic coast.

I remember the journey to Bologna well. After driving down to London Victoria in our old grey Morris Minor JDO 159, the tears in my eyes would be welling up as we approached the platform where I knew we'd be saying goodbye to Dad. By the time the train neared Dover though, I'd more or less cheered up – knowing that in the evening of the following day I'd be running into the arms of all my family in Bologna. At Dover our ferry (which was for years the *SS Invicta*) would be waiting for us.

The crossing to Calais took about an hour-and-a-half. Disembarking was always a fretful time trying to find the right couchette carriage on the right train. Then we'd start off on the seemingly endless journey through France and Switzerland to Bologna. Hour upon hour through France, it would be clickety-clack, clackety-click – with the inevitable upheaval in the evening when the guard came round with the key to unlock all the folding seats that converted into couchettes. Pillows, sheets and blankets were handed out and we would all settle down for the night.

As I write, my eyes become heavy just remembering those hours of half-sleep as if time was being dragged through treacle. Every now and then I'd wake, surprised that the train was going backwards. It was only after a number of years that I understood what everyone had told me – the train, having pulled into a station, had to reverse out to continue the journey several miles back along the track. A ridiculous notion to a young mind of course, but at the time it all added to the monotony of the clickety-clack which in itself was only relieved at intervals when the train went over a level crossing. The strangely smooth passage over one of these, with bells madly jingling off in the distance, gave me the impression we were heading in the right direction and not going back to Calais.

Sometime during the night the temperature would drop noticeably and the air would become sharp and crisp as we approached the Alps. We'd pass through the St Gotthard Tunnel and the journey would take on a different feel as the train headed off through Switzerland, then around and past Lake Lugano and Lake Como, then on the last stretch through Milano, Piacenza, Parma and Modena. At last we'd arrive at Bologna where I'd already be leaning out of the window waiting to catch the first glimpse of all our family waiting on the platform.

I could not even begin to describe the happiness of the next six weeks, tempered by the agonising wait for Dad's arrival for the last two. In the days before fishing took hold and my mind became awash with Mitchells and porcupine quills, my mornings were spent impatiently waiting for the postman. On hearing the bell, I'd go flying down the stairs to the street in the hope he'd be handing me the brown paper roll with Dad's familiar writing on the side: Leda Pledger, ℅ Ginghini, Via Begatto 3, Bologna, Italy. I'd feverishly cut it open and there inside were my comics from home – *Buster* and *Valiant*. Then I'd rush off to lie on the bed reading all the latest adventures of my heroes, The Steel Claw and Captain Hurricane and, in particular, the best of them all, Kelly's Eye.

Trying to choose a few memories from so many would be almost as pointless as trying to count the stars, but the overriding constants in all of them were twofold – the desire to draw, and the happiness I felt whenever I was near water. The need to draw and paint like my dear Zio Sergio, himself an accomplished artist, must certainly be why I always aspired to be like him. Sergio was a truly handsome man, much like Dean Martin, but in character the quietest, most laid-back person I've ever known. His great love of art and cartoons has, I am pleased to say, filtered through me into my children, Douglas and Laura, and every time I look at them I can see him.

I was at my happiest when I was with all my family a short drive into the countryside, playing by the many rocky streams and watching wagtails, serins and red-backed shrikes through Dad's binoculars. Returning home, I would spend hours sitting at a big marble table beside an old open window, drawing birds. The window had ancient wooden shutters and floor-length silk curtains, the curtains heralding each welcome breeze by billowing all around me in the days of suffocating heat.

From deep within my sixpence jar of memories of Bologna, I pick one which certainly must be one of my very first, as I could only have been two years old or so. I am beginning to realise that my most vivid memories almost always concern water. Mum and I were with Laura and Sergio, walking back from the big Cimitero (the cemetery) alongside which ran the old local canal. The canal ran through some wild ground (there were many such areas in and around Bologna for many years after the war), and I always held someone's hand tightly – usually Sergio's – as we followed the banks. The canal both fascinated and frightened me. Every year the water, highly coloured, raced by, turgid and brown with a peculiar smell. Nothing lived in it. When I returned years later though, I found my old friend running clear, with billowing fronds of streamer weed and, keeping the butterflies company, shoals of rising, dimpling fish. They must have been chub.

Another memory with which I was rewarded was finding a giant peacock moth, wings extended, resting up in some grass at the base of an old telegraph pole. I remembered it as being the size of a small plate, which wasn't too far out as it is the largest European moth with an incredible wingspan of six inches.

From the time I could walk the magic of fishing was slowly yet imperceptibly drawing me in. In the centre of Bologna are the Giardini Margherita, a twenty minute walk along Via Guerrazzi from Nonna's

house. Situated just outside Porta Castiglione (one of ten remaining ancient *porte* or gateways that linked the old wall encircling the old centre of the city), these gardens are a wonderful parkland within easy reach of everyone living in the crowded, jumbled, streets. Within the parkland, near an enclosure housing deer and just next door to a couple of lions, was a small ornamental lake, along one side of which was a funny higgledy-piggledy wall. This meandering wall, about thirty yards long and three feet high, was made of jagged quartz and dropped down eight feet or so into the water. Along here gathered the local children, mostly young boys, who leant over the wall with hand lines, shiny red plastic bobbers and small hooks on which were moulded little pellets of chewed bread.

Mirroring the image of the rows of young faces looking directly down into the water below were gatherings of tiny little goldfish, looking up.

While I was too small to join in the fishing, Mum would hold me up so I could look down at the little fish. I was fascinated, watching for ripples that would suddenly circle out from the tiny floats. My heart racing, my eyes were opened to another world, tantalisingly just out of reach.

From when I was five or six years old, and up to about the age of ten, Athos and Dad would take me to a pebbly little stream just outside Bologna which was flanked by western balsams. Surrounded by their magical scent, I used to dam up the stream with rocks and spend the afternoon splashing around as the water rose. Once I was overjoyed that a couple of small fish ended up stranded in my little pool with me. If all this wasn't special enough, I remember sitting with Dad and Athos on the rocks as I dried out in the sun, eating a panino with prosciutto or salamino, and drinking San Pelegrino Aranciata from one of those funny-shaped bottles. Utter contentment.

Waking early in cotton sheets on those lovely fresh mornings, I would be out of my mind waiting for Dad to take me out into the old centre of Bologna. We'd spend hours there taking photos and walking around all the 'back doubles' as Dad called them. By mid-morning the centre of town had come to life; the cool mornings had given way to stifling heat, and in the incessant hustle and bustle, myriads of glittering particles of dust could be seen floating and dancing in rays of burning sunlight, cascading round every corner. As we walked, the smell of fresh-baked bread and coffee from various shop doorways added to the general hubbub and atmosphere of Bologna waking up.

We'd spend much of our time searching for fishing shops. Not in those days for fishing tackle, but for stuffed birds, which were traditionally used to decorate the window displays. It is almost impossible to explain just how much I desired stuffed birds in those early years, but up until the age of twelve or so, just about all my waking thoughts were of them, and probably most of my dreams. Watching birds, drawing birds, photographing birds, and living in eternal hope that someone would buy me one of the stuffed birds that I'd set my heart on.

So my heart would beat faster as we searched Dad's back doubles. I remember the sadness I always felt as we passed the fishmonger's shop, trying not to look at the live eels writhing in a big ceramic white tub under the big bench on which all the fish were on show. I can remember wanting to save up my money so I could buy a few of the eels, then get Dad to take me along to the nearest river to let them go. I think it must be why I have sympathetic feelings towards eels even today. Something my friends have never shared.

By the time I was nudging thirteen, fishing began taking hold, and I was beginning to tread our well-worn paths through Bologna on my own. Any excuse and I'd be out, walking miles round the old city centre, or catching buses further afield, to buy a simple tub of split-shot, a spool of line or yet another couple of porcupine quills.

Italian fishing shops had an indescribable pull on me. Where once my head was filled with stuffed birds, now virtually every waking moment was spent thinking about the most inconsequential item of tackle, then deciding and planning which tackle shop to go and buy it from. Even now I can picture and place those shops in order of desirability. Who had the best assortment of floats; which sold Platil Strong line; which had the best selection of rods. And, most important, which sold Mitchells.

I am, like every fisherman I've met before or since, hooked on Mitchells. My first was a much loved, much used, Mitchell 314. But only a year after I'd got it, my tongue was hanging out for, to my mind, the most outlandishly desirable reel of all – the tiny Mitchell 308.

The little shop at Casalecchio, just outside Bologna past Aunty Laura's and Uncle Sergio's home had, I was told, a Mitchell 308. Casalecchio was a little town through which ran the River Reno. The Reno was a rocky, pebbly, river, very shallow, in some years almost dried-up, and it was where Dad and I used to watch every European species of wagtail there is. And where, on that day of days after we'd watched and photographed strawberry finches nesting in some tall reeds, I actually saw, for a few seconds through Dad's binoculars, a wryneck perch up on top of a bamboo cane. I would not swap that memory for anything.

And from the shop, not a hundred yards away from the very spot I saw the wryneck, I bought my little Mitchell 308.

On the crowded bus ride back, cramped amongst a million passengers who I knew were all looking at me, I proudly unpacked and repacked the little reel from its big black plastic box, unpacked it again, wound the handle, clicked over the bail arm, wound it some more, folded the handle, put it back. Opened it up, unfolded the handle …

Returning home, by the window on the marble table, I filled the two spools with line, and spent the entire day fussing over it, winding it, polishing it, placing it in front of my art pad and drawing it. Quite simply, no other reel in the world could take the place of that little 308. Even now, matched with a tiny cane rod or a carbon wand, a few hooks and a can of worms, I could catch you any fish that swims. What need would there be for anything else? With that little reel I can make magic happen.

A five minute walk from Nonna's house in Via Begatto in the other direction, was a tiny little fishing shop. It found me while I was passing one day to go elsewhere. It was shut though. It was dark and forbidding with a few pike skulls in the window. It had the look of always having been there. The window fittings, the shutters, the door, all had the appearance of having aged at the same time as the crumbly old walls surrounding them. Over numerous days I returned time and again but it was always shut. Not closed, just shut. I almost gave up on it, but one day, for no reason that was obvious, the door was open, so I went in. A little old lady, a very little, very frail, little white-haired, old lady, whose age I guessed must have

been easily equal to the surrounding walls was busy behind the counter. Hunched over, nose pressed close to her trembly old hands, and totally oblivious to me standing there, she sat whipping hooks. So I just stood there and let my eyes wander around the dusty, dark old shelves. There were some more pike skulls, an old glass tumbler in which were several small porcupine quills, and upon the top shelf far away from any sunlight and completely unnoticed or forgotten by every previous customer, but not it seems by the spiders (a thick layer of cobwebs was draped all over it), was that old familiar black plastic box. But this time holding the Holy Grail: a Mitchell 408.

Did I really need another reel? Did I consider at all what Mum and Dad would say about me even thinking of buying another one? No and no again.

But there was no home, other than mine, where that reel was going to live.

The little old lady dusted off the box, and while she was muttering that she didn't even know it was up there, I paid with the just-enough money I had on me and left her to her hook-tying. I like to think that even now, as I write forty-three years later, she's still there – probably covered in as many cobwebs as the little 408 was that day, but still there. Whipping hooks.

Bologna fishing shops forty years ago were wonderful places. Invisible hands pulled me inside and left me standing there with eyes flickering around, mentally listing everything I needed, wanted, didn't really need, or was going to buy anyway just because I couldn't buy it back home in England. Quite why I bought the big black-and-yellow rubber wasp with the ridiculous plastic wings, moulded on a size six hook, I have no idea. Nor the immense, brown rubber crayfish that had, shoved through it, an equally huge bronze double hook which, if truth be told, would've held up anything in Dad's shed. Neither of them ever got used, but long after I lost the wasp I found the crayfish, which had spent its entire life nestling in one of the dark corners of my tackle box. At some stage it had melted into an uncrayfish-like lump: a sticky blob, with a couple of beady rubber eyes peering out from between what was left of its twangy feelers.

The loss of the wasp, coinciding with a few days of an over-inventive mind and bugger all else to do, had me capturing a load of bluebottles and keeping them in a jar until the whole lot died. I then set about attempting to tie each with cotton to some lovely silver spade-end hooks. Long, long after, I really should've given the idea up as one of the most pointless things I had ever done and, surrounded by assorted silver spades with a multitude of glued and tied-on smashed-up wings and legs, I ended up with one implausibly, superbly mounted bluebottle. But I'd obviously used up any vestige of intelligence I had at the time, as a couple of days later after I'd placed this masterpiece in an old sweet tin and left it to bang around in my tackle box, I opened it up and found the thing smashed to pieces.

It was around this time that Sergio told me of a little lake called Lago Barca (Boat Lake) a short bus ride from his home. Between the time he told me of the lake and the day Dad agreed to take me there, I don't think I slept at all. The only thing I did manage to do was find a tackle shop that had a big two-pint plastic bait box in stock. Then, in almost-incoherent Italian, got the owner to understand enough to fill the thing up with maggots. Probably the part he understood most of all, was to fill it up completely. Returning home, I placed it in the corner of a cool room while we all went out for the day. Not realising the room didn't stay cool during the afternoons, we arrived back some time later to find, in the intense heat, that the over-filled bait box had given up trying to contain the forty million maggots and the lid had blown off.

Another sleepless night, and the following day, after a sweltering two-bus journey across Bologna, Dad and I finally found ourselves standing on the gravel banks of Lago Barca. (Should anyone ever ask me which two lakes would be my favourite places in the whole world to watch a float, it would be the lake at Barclay Park in Hoddesdon and the little lake we were now looking at.) Dad paid the few hundred Lire day ticket and we ambled off to sit under some balsam poplars on the opposite bank.

I set up my three-piece hollow glass match rod, which we'd brought with us to Italy, and the little 308, then laid a couple of maggots on the bottom (which was perhaps eight feet deep) under one of my diminutive porcupine quills. I was absolutely confident of immediate success, but despondency started to creep in as we noticed other anglers catching fish with a regularity that began to irk. After longer than I would have liked my little float gave a couple of slight digs, lifted slightly, cocked and slid under. Unlike the other anglers' fish (which were a few ounces at most), on the strike, my fish, a carp, tore off and then just blundered around the lake in front of me, not showing any inclination whatsoever of coming to the net. With only one-and-a-half pound line and a size 18 hook between myself and what I'd unbelievably hooked into, it wasn't until a further twenty minutes had gone by that we began to think I might actually land it. Dad stood behind me taking a series of photos while a gallery of people came to join in and watch what was going on.

Eventually the fish – a glorious common carp – was slid into the net and then lovingly placed on the grass at the water's edge. Photographed it weighed-in at an incredible five pounds and must remain as one of my most memorable captures. The gallery of onlookers, all local anglers, stood in disbelief as Dad and I gently released the fish. Whereas most of the locals continued to be irritated by 'the mad Englishmen' at our release of carp over subsequent trips, one or two perhaps envious of our notoriety and the attention we were getting, began to release their own fish. The sad thing about Italian fishing at the time was that anything caught stayed caught.

On our next few trips we caught two more commons of 4 lb 8 oz and 1 lb 12 oz respectively and mirror carp of 14 oz and 2 lb.

The association of western balsam poplars with everything wonderful in my world was further enhanced many years later when I discovered through the writings of Chris Yates, that in the early days of Redmire, twin balsams bathed the pool in their heady aroma. I smile when I realise that friends I've never personally met or known, anglers I've admired and loved through their writings, BB, Maurice Ingham, Dick Walker, Pete Thomas and Chris himself, have all shared some of our happiest moments breathing the aromatic air surrounding them.

Basil Ede

IN 1965, WHEN I was ten years old, *Country Life* published Basil Ede's *Birds Of Town and Village*. At six guineas it was way too expensive to buy, so out of necessity I continually renewed it from Hoddesdon Library. Although Arthur Singer's book, *Birds of the World*, ran it a close second, no other book has influenced me throughout my life as Basil Ede's has.

Looking back through eyes of a ten-year-old, I remember how I lived in awe of the impossible beauty of his paintings. Just as I do now.

I turned eleven on May 17 the following year. Words cannot describe what I was feeling as I unwrapped my present. I just *knew* what it was. I was so familiar with the feeling of the book, it mattered little how much Mum and Dad had tried to disguise it in layers of wrapping – my very own copy of *Birds of Town and Village*. Strangely I was actually quite sad to see the library book go, especially with all my familiar renewal dates littering the inside cover. But owning my very own copy, that was something else. It must have given me extra confidence in my own little pencil drawings – enough to ask Mum and Dad if it would be okay for me to write to Basil Ede.

Including five of my little drawings I'd copied from Arthur Singer's book, I wrote Basil Ede a letter. Incredibly, a couple of weeks later I got a reply.

Dear Maurice.

1st December 1966

   Thank you very much for your nice letter. I am sorry I was unable to reply immediately but I wanted to have a little time to study the drawings you sent. I think these are very good indeed. I particularly like the Grebe which is very characteristic of the bird.

   Now, if you are asking for my criticism, do not be disappointed or offended at anything I may say — in any case I shall criticise in very general terms. In the first place try to confine your work to birds with which you are completely familiar. Stuffed birds are a very good aid — but only an aid for plumage detail. It is still essential to know the bird in real life because, as you know, they have their own characteristic movements which one must try to convey in one's painting or drawing. In order to do this successfully it helps if you can get a good idea of the bone structure so that — even without a model to work from you can place a wing or foot in any position you choose — consistent with what you have seen in real life. Here is a typical wing construction (you might compare it to a human arm):-

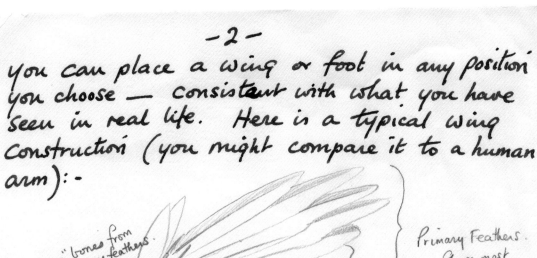

"Finger" bones from which primary feathers radiate

Wrist

SHOULDER.

Primary Feathers.
9 on most.
10 on larger birds

Secondary Feathers.
9 on most birds

—and the leg of a bird roughly like this

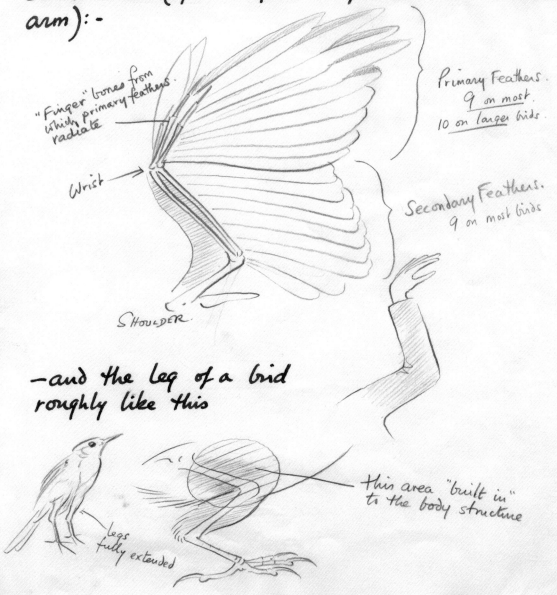

this area "built in" to the body structure

legs fully extended

30

Now, in your drawings, you are using a somewhat 'tight' technique. I suggest you start work on a larger scale — get used to doing so from the word go. Find out from your specimens or books the measurements and <u>draw, when possible with smaller birds, to life size.</u> Obviously you cannot do this with Golden Eagles, Ospreys etc. By making the drawings larger you are giving yourself more freedom of movement with brush or pencil. Incidentally the illustrations in "Birds of Town & Village" are with one or two exceptions two-thirds life size. The Marsh & Coal Tits, Robin & Dunnock, Long-tailed Tits are about three-quarters life size.

When you start painting you must pay a lot of attention to light and shade. I use a tinted paper which lets me emphasise this — and I mix all the colours with Chinese white paint which is worked fairly heavily on the paper to obscure the background colour. The highlights and actual white feathers are painted using WINDSOR & NEWTONS PERMANENT WHITE designer's gouache. They also make Chinese white but they call it <u>ZINC WHITE</u> and it allows the colours to show through when mixed. You will need to do a lot of practice and, whilst referring to the work of other artists (to see how they have tackled various problems) try not to stop your own individual ideas coming to the fore.

You will need good brushes to get good results (I am not a believer in the saying - "bad workmen always blame their tools") for without good materials you cannot hope to get good results. Brushes are expensive so take care you do not "scrub" them about when charging them with paint —and always see they are well washed and re-pointed (with the mouth) before putting them away.

I do not know if all this helps you in any way — but I do hope so. I am returning the drawings to you. Thank you for letting me see them. By the way they were a little bent at the corners when they arrived so, when sending work anywhere, be sure and pack them between pieces of stiff board.

I thought you might be interested to
have a copy of the catalogue for a recent
exhibition I had in New York. The Owl's
head on the cover (Great Horned Owl) may
reveal some points of brush technique for you
as it is enlarged up from the original.

Good luck —and do not despair if
things to not go well at first.

Yours Sincerely

David Ede

I'd always wanted to paint like Uncle Sergio, who preferred painting scenes of the mountains he loved, and still-life oil paintings of copper pots and pans. I'd already tried my hand with a set of poster paints Mum and Dad had bought me, contenting myself for a while with copying Sergio's style, and for some reason concentrating on clouds. But, spurred-on by Basil Ede's encouragement, I began to feel the need to add colour to my own little pencil drawings of birds.

It wasn't too long, though, before my love of fishing began to creep in and I started to include paintings of fish in my repertoire. The first fish I tried was a brown trout – not because I was particularly fond of them, but thanks to all the markings down the sides, I felt I they were simpler to paint as I didn't need to laboriously paint a million scales. My next attempt was of a chub.

While all this was going on, Dad had been in contact with a taxidermist in London, a Mr Eric Hare. Eric was employed by the great taxidermists, Rowland Ward, and was not only a great craftsman with birds and animals, but fish too. And to my joy, one dismal rainy evening, Dad took me over to meet him at his home in Golders Green.

I was beside myself with anticipation as we entered the house and I wasn't disappointed with the rest of the evening. Given my Dad's wages at the time, he must have nearly bankrupted himself as he agreed to buy a little dunlin and ringed plover for me and then spent an additional £10 for an immaculately restored Victorian woodcock*. Just before we left Eric showed us a 25 lb pike he was working on, and truly the effect it had on me was indescribable so I won't even try. Eric could see how taken I was with birds, paintings and fish so he suggested we go and see a good friend of his, Aylmer Tryon.

Arranging yet another meeting, Mum and Dad took me to see Mr Tryon who not only owned the famous art gallery in Dover Street, London, but was a legendary fisherman to boot. We took along a few of my little drawings and the paintings of the chub and trout. Unbelievably, like Basil Ede, Mr Tryon gave freely of his time and walked us around his gallery, showing us original paintings by Argentinian artist Axel Amuchastegui as well as Basil Ede. I remember standing in silence, completely overwhelmed at being in the presence of the man who'd caught one of the legendary three 14 lb 6 oz barbel which held the-then British record, and Basil Ede's original paintings at the same time.

Showing genuine interest in my paintings, Mr Tryon kept the chub and trout to show to some friends and a few days later he phoned to say he'd sold the trout for £10.

Although this little window is only one of the many that look out on the path I've taken with my art, these memories will remain among my most cherished. The love, faith and encouragement given to me by my parents and the time and generous attention shown to me by Basil Ede, one of the world's greatest bird artists, will always guide every brush stroke.

---

* Later, as a thank you to my Dad, I brought the woodcock back to life when I used it as a model for a painting in my book, *Game Birds*, published by Collins in 1981.

Dave Evans and my brother, Doug

Colin Nobes and me

Barry Waterman

Me, Vince Cawley, Steve Tibble and Scott Poynter

NO FISHING

FRIENDSHIP

As time trundles on I find the things I can most easily recall concern the company of friends and the little incidents which are tinged with the ridiculous.

Don't Look Up

BEING BLESSED WITH an ability to gravitate towards the absurd, like a magician I can conjure up ridiculous situations at will and with a wisp of smoke from my fingertips all manner of delights can appear. (Although I freely admit that most of what does appear is completely out of control; my raggedy collection of dear friends over the years will readily testify to this.) I've shared moments with them to almost overflow the sixpence jar, and moments that, if I were to be completely honest, I could happily forget.

Like the day when an early mate called Pete came up with the best explanation ever as I lay on the grass with my nose bleeding as if it had been opened up with a shovel. We were about seven. A few minutes prior to me lying on the ground screaming, I'd been happily running through the grass waving my arms around, when from out of nowhere, a big round stone smashed into the side of my nose with so much force I was sent flying backwards. As he dragged me off back home in a trail of blood, Pete said:

'You've been hit by a meteorite.'

Weather or Not

JANUARY 5TH, 1970. We were both fourteen-years-old at the time. The day had nothing going for it, even before I'd opened the front door. It was freezing, pitch black and the snow was already piling up when I peeked out to see Vince, after a long walk from his house, standing under a mountain of tackle, covered in snow. Walking past haloed streetlights through the white ghost town that was Hoddesdon at that insane hour of the morning, we arrived at the bus stop and waited for the first one of the day, which was to take us to Turnford. It was still completely dark, even after the endlessly slow trudge along Slipe Lane down to King's Weir. And it remained so as we tramped along the towpath to Aqueduct Lock, past the lock house, then on to the river. And it snowed and snowed. Apart from the bus driver who must have been part owl, there was no one else around to question our logic of even thinking of getting out of a warm bed – much less doing so.

As we fished the day away, the snow gave way to rain, and the whole landscape around us melted into a slop bath of liquid mud. Vince sat a few yards downstream of me perched, like me, on top of the eight foot high bank. A stand of tall bushes and trees between us, we both cast across gravelly shallows to where I, at least, began to get the odd bite on legered lobworms. The conditions were impossible. The only place where there wasn't any mud was in the river itself, so I decided to clamber down the sloping bank and set up my folding chair actually in the water about six feet out – the river there being about a foot deep. I could just make out Vince's swim through the bushes, although all I could see of Vince himself was a pair of knees poking out from under an umbrella which he'd wedged into the sloping bank, precariously perched about three feet from the top of the ridge. My swim proved to be a little easier to fish, and although sitting in the river was creating its own problems, at least I began to hit a few bites. While Vince just sat, huddled up, not daring to move.

Hitting my next bite, I think I must have pressed some kind of red button which unleashed things we really could have done without.

'Here Vince, I think this one's pretty big. I might need a hand.'

(In the long list of things I wish I'd never said, this probably must rate at number two or number three. Maybe even number one.)

Given that I was now playing the largest chub I'd ever hooked, 2½ lb as it turned out, I hadn't noticed how Vince was faring. But apparently he'd successfully negotiated himself out from under his umbrella and started to clamber up to the top of Mudbath Ridge when he toppled face first into it. Managing to get to his feet again he collected his extending landing net, progressed a couple of steps and fell over once more. Thinking better of asking him to prolong the torture, I said:

'It's okay mate, I'll do it myself.'

Muttering to himself, he skidded and slid back. After landing and releasing the chub on my own, I cast out and caught another one – this one about a pound. I could sense Vince was getting the hump and suggested, not for the first time in my life, we swap swims.

He collected his rod and amazingly made it to the top of the bank behind my swim. And, with the agility of a mountain goat, I simply walked up past him with my rod in hand and waited for him to descend down to where my chair was – tantalisingly close and clean in the water. He made one step forward, lost any equilibrium he was ever born with and flew down the mudslide on his back. Standing upright, half-in half-out of the water, and looking like something that had clambered out of a B Western mud fight, he looked at me and said:

'I can't sit on your chair in this state. I'm covered in mud.'

At which point I replied:

'Don't worry, fold the back rest down and sit on that.'

Picking his rod up from underwater, he folded the back down, sat on it, and the back legs gave way. The whole lot – chair, rod, Vince – just folded up and went right into the river. Plus, as he went, he kicked in my bait box of maggots as well.

As I ran down past him to save the maggot box, which was sailing away in the current, my hat fell off and began to sink. As I retrieved them both with a rod rest, Vince loudly announced to me, and to anyone within maybe a quarter of a mile, in language that would have gained him free entry through the Gates of Hell, that he was going home. He then threw his rod up the bank, which of course got stuck in the trees. Then, while wrenching it out, the line snapped.

As I sat back in my chair, trying to make sense of things, I glanced along the bank to where Vince had disappeared behind the bushes and was treated to the sight of a missile of mud about the size of a cake tin, hurtling through the air and landing midway out in the river right in the centre of my swim. The cataclysmic splash drowned out most of what he was shouting.

He packed up, left me there and went home. I gave it another half hour and packed up myself. Taking an age to walk back to the main road, which must have been easily a mile-and-a-half away, it was already dark by the time I arrived at the bus stop.

It was only later – a lot later – when I phoned Vince to see what had happened to him, he informed me that given the state he was in, there was no way on earth he would ever be allowed on a bus, so he just walked home.

To those of you reading this who don't know how far it is from below Aqueduct Lock in Turnford, to Westfield Road in Hoddesdon, I can only tell you it's a long, long way. Flying crows would not have seen him, as his zig-zag route was probably in the region of seven or eight miles.

Will the Real Steve Arnold Please Stand Up

THE MILL POOL was surrounded by a jumbled mess of old sheds which had fallen into a state of disrepair. And, as with all neglected little fisheries, the place had Vince and me by the throat. Just behind St. Augustine's Church in Broxbourne, the mill had stood for over nine hundred years and was listed in the Domesday Book. It ceased milling in 1891 and was used for a variety of purposes until it was almost completely destroyed by fire on October 1, 1949. Not that any of this history was of much interest to either of us – we just wanted to fish the mill pool. It was very fishy, fed by a gushing stream from the millstream flowing above, on its way to where it joined the River Lea opposite the Crown pub on the other bank.

Sadly, fishing the mill pool was closed to all who were not members of Lychnobite A.S. so looking at it was as near as we usually got. Luckily, though, a schoolmate of ours, Steve Arnold, was a member and because he was smaller than Vince he was easily persuaded to part with his ticket for a day.

February 22, 1970 was grey, miserable and rainy. Never wanting to fish apart, we elected to fish side by side on the most ridiculously small ledge built into the right-hand wall where the water gushed past. Measuring probably only 1 ft x 4 ft wide, I am still at a loss as to how we managed it with all our tackle. The ledge is still there and anyone wanting to see the spot can still do so. As I write, ivy has taken over and there's a small bramble bush growing on it, and it only takes wrens and blue tits two or three seconds to get bored with the lack of space before they flit off across the pool.

We fished for a while and although Vince brought a gudgeon to the surface, he foolishly let it swim around for a bit while he finished his coffee, hoping it would fall off. It swam into a rock and he had to pull for a break – something I delight in reminding him of every now and then. Fed-up with catching nothing more for a while we decided to fish off the bank

41

amongst a jungle of assorted planks of wood, pallets and God-knows-what-else. Vince chose to fish the next swim down from the wall, precariously balancing the legs of his stool on a half-submerged slatted piece of fence. I fancied a spot a little further along which I could only get to by negotiating around a load of floating wood. After an age we began to fish. The bailiff arrived and asked to see his ticket. Vince handed him the thing on which was written the words, Steve Arnold.

Seemingly happy enough with that, the bailiff called over to me:

'Can I see your ticket son?'

I made some struggling type movements and told him I couldn't move.

'What's your name then?'

'Steve Arnold.'

Faced with two Steve Arnolds on top of the one he probably already knew, I think we must have caught him on a good day. Either that or he thought leaving us to finish the day in worsening conditions was punishment enough. Worsen they certainly did. Someone came over to the sluice from the millstream, opened it up, and within minutes the surge of floodwater turned the whole pool into a swirling bowl of oxtail soup. Although I'd caught a lovely roach of eight inches, the rising water suggested I'd better put a leger out. The heaviest I'd got was an eighth-of-an-ounce, so I threaded it up with a single maggot on a size 16 and flicked it out. I don't remember the bite but all of a sudden I was playing a heavy fish which, after a hair-raising fight in amongst the floating wood, turned out to be a glorious mid-winter tench of 1 lb 12 oz which should still have been sleeping off the cold weather. Obviously wakened by the massive surge of water, it must have felt the need to pick at a maggot before the current made good its threat of sending the maggot, the tench itself, the log-jam of wood and everything else in the pool down into the Crown Pub.

I just had to have a photograph of my superb tench, so I decided I'd have to run to Broxbourne, find a telephone box, phone Dad and get him to come down with the camera. While I was deliberating which was to be my last cast before heading off to town, Vince caught a small roach and foolishly leaned over to pop it into his keepnet. Straightening up on his stool, he caught the back of his boot on something and, shoving his hand in the groundbait, went flying backwards into the pool. At one point his head was completely under water, like a trapped upside-down turtle, and no amount of arm or leg flailing did any good. It was even an effort for me to get over to him, but after what must have seemed to him an age, I managed it. With a bit of help he surfaced looking like the twin brother of the creature from the Black Lagoon and in this guise he shook the water off and carried on fishing while I ran off to phone Dad. A half-an-hour later I returned and joined 'the creature' to eke out a few last casts before Dad arrived. Ten minutes later Dad turned up and the excitement in his eyes as he took those lovely old black and white photos of my big tench add the extra magic to my memories forty-two years on as I look through the pages of my old fishing album.

The Stort Unfished

NEW YEAR'S EVE, 1970, at St Monica's Priory in Hoddesdon.

I don't know who made the biggest mistake, Chad for inviting us or Vince and I for accepting. Anyway, no matter – the three of us were now at the party. I have no idea whose party it was, nor did I know any of the dozens of people who were whooping it up in the great hall. We'd all turned fifteen in the preceding year and although Chad and Vince were already accustomed to drinking, I most certainly wasn't. The hardest stuff I'd swallowed up to then was Tizer.

We had planned a pre-dawn fishing excursion for the following morning, our intention being a day on the Stort next door to Rye House Sewage Farm, and I guess the party was just a way to use up some time before the main objective – fishing. I don't remember the exact moment things started to unravel but I have a sneaky suspicion it was maybe when the other two headed off to the bar to get a drink. As they returned, grinning, they handed me a glass. Subsequent questioning revealed it was half-a-pint of cider. Already familiar with the smell of it as Dad used to drink it with his dinner on Sundays, I detested the stuff and told them so. However because of this they suggested I drink it in one go. This I did and was immediately handed another one. Unknown to me, this one had an inch-and-a-half of gin hidden inside it. So did the next. Miraculously nothing much seemed to be happening, so for reasons best known to my two dubiously good friends, the next one contained a quarter-of-a-pint of gin, and shortly afterwards their grinning faces seemed to be curiously sliding off the screen.

Heading off to find the bathroom, I seem to remember trying to negotiate a tiled hallway which at the time looked to be as wide as our back garden. For some reason my legs weren't functioning correctly and I do remember having to lean on both walls several times before I found the stairs and, quite miraculously, the bathroom.

As I opened my eyes, I wondered why I was lying in a large white bath, when I was only trying to find the toilet. The next thing I remember was Mum opening the front door as I half fell inside. Apparently Chad and Vince had taken me home and then went back to the party, eventually making it back home themselves at about half-past-three the following morning, New Year's Day.

When my bed stopped floating and rolling long enough for me to actually wake up it was 7 a.m. Strangely I felt fine. Having heard all about hangovers this seemed no big deal – in fact I felt fresh as a daisy. Best I'd ever been. I rushed downstairs, picked up the phone and woke Vince, who no doubt was only just getting off to sleep. I informed him I felt super wonderful and within twenty minutes I'd be ready to go fishing. I took it that the slurred reply was in the positive so, putting down the phone, I walked into the kitchen …

The next time I woke it was strangely dark, and opening the curtains, it was the same outside. Falling back into bed, the next time I drew the curtains it was already 2 January and half-way through the morning. The initiation into the world of alcohol was wasted on me and it taught me to steer clear of the stuff – if only because, like homework, exams and girls, it got in the way of fishing.

Not So Dedicated Followers of Fashion

GIVEN THE SLIGHTLY off-the-wall nature of our little band, it's inevitable that on occasions, especially when the fish seemed to be asleep, our trips descended into the absurd.

Like the day when Vince decided to see if he could shove a whole packet of Trebor Extra Strong mints into his mouth. Incredibly he managed it, and after a lot of crunching and frothing, he swallowed the lot. Then he drank a pint of ice-cold water and nearly blew his eyes out.

The food we took fishing followed the same downward-spiralling path, and it's not wholly surprising that my stomach couldn't always keep up

with it all. Packets of Lovehearts and Flying Saucers, Jamboree Bags, Cherry Bitters and Victory V's all made nice additions to the scotch eggs, Marmite sandwiches (with Ryvita crackers and butter shoved into them) and bottles of Tizer and cherryade which made up the wholesome part of the diet.

Our quest for sartorial elegance also had a long way to go. In fact it had a long way to go nowhere. How on earth Vince and I got away with wearing what we did in the fourth year at Broxbourne School, I'll never know. While I continually rounded off my school uniform with tasselled cowboy boots, Vince was going through his Ben Sherman shirt, Staypress trousers and Royals stage. Looking increasingly like a deranged cross between Alexei Sayle and Uncle Fester of the Addams Family, he took on a strangely Las Vegas look on our fishing trips when he added Elvis sunglasses. Probably the most idiotic thing I had to sit through was watching Vince's routine when cleaning his shades. First, he'd snap out one lens, putting the glasses back on while he polished it. Then he'd turn to me, grinning – one lens in, one out, then snap the first back in, and repeat the whole thing with the second. The whole performance would last a couple of minutes and was usually finished off with a leisurely amble along the bank practising his John Wayne walk which, depending on irregularities on the bank, sometimes looked more like a Robert Mitchum walk. I'll never forget the day I was round at Vince's watching *The Intelligence Men*, a film featuring Morecambe and Wise. In one particular scene they're both walking up and down arguing over whose walk looked more like John Wayne's and whose, Robert Mitchum's.

If nothing else we were in good company.

The path of fashion ran neither true nor particularly long, and it's interesting how my sense of fashion seemed to follow what they were wearing in Hollywood. Or rather what they were wearing in certain Hollywood movies. The desire to impress a girlfriend led me to buy (for 50p at the Hoddesdon Methodist church rummage sale) a tiny little corduroy jacket, which looked just like the one Glenn Ford had on in westerns like *The Sheepman* (1958) and *3:10 to Yuma* (1957). I first wore it on 17 July, 1971, when Chad, Vince and I went night fishing at Barclay Park. I'd convinced myself that shivering uncontrollably in that little corduroy jacket might warm me up a bit rather than run home the five hundred yards or so to get something more appropriate, but no, apparently not. Thinking of how many hundreds of miles Glenn travelled across Arizona and how warm he looked on those cold desert nights on the telly, had me thinking, seriously there must be another way.

Which leads directly to my two pork pie hats – one brown, one black.

There will be those of you familiar with the long sorry tale of my brown pork pie hat. In my previous book I wrote about the fate which befell it, in what I can only refer to as the 'Infamous Greek Meat Slicer Incident'. For quite some time though, the black hat accompanied me in all its magnificent un-butchered finery on most of my fishing trips – my friends becoming resigned and then even accustomed to it.

Sadly though this black hat one day made the acquaintance of Pigeon, a cute, fluffy little hamster my daughter Laura had bought me. Pigeon, not feeling that she had enough toys to play with, or wheels or balls to keep her interested, decided to take full advantage of my rather lax understanding of what hamsters are capable of. She decided, all on her own, that a more fun alternative was to crane her head through the bars of her cage and chew the living daylights out of the brim of my remaining black hat into what they call in the old Westerns, 'doll rags'.

So far from being remotely like anything Gene Hackman ever wore in *The French Connection*, it has now joined the brown hat in having the provenance of something from a good local Hammer horror film.

Return of 'Torchy the Battery Boy'

AS TIME TRUNDLES on I find the things I can most easily recall concern the company of friends and little incidents which are tinged with the ridiculous can transport me back to those long lost black and white days when I used to watch The Woodentops, Twizzle, and Torchy The Battery Boy on our old television set. I can look back through my old records and remember no end of catches of large fish, but the sparkly-twinkly memories which need no prompting from old diaries, are always there. Precious little jewels which are remembered with great fondness.

Like the summer evening quite some years ago when Scotty and I were sitting, as usual, side-by-side, tench fishing at Toyhall, our club lake in Cheshunt. We weren't doing anything in particular; I know I was just sitting there happily watching my float, and I think Scotty was fumbling with something as he arranged a few bits and pieces in the failing light. All of a sudden there was an explosion in his face and he went flying off backwards into the brambles. He'd been holding his mini Maglite torch clamped between his teeth and it blew up in his face. Quite what the hell happened neither of us knew, but as he went to pick it up, he couldn't – it was red hot.

Then there was the huge barbel (which looked to be about twelve or thirteen pounds) that we discovered sometime around 1990. It lived in and below the staggered weir at Hartham Common in Hertford. We named it 'Whitespot' because of a large patch of light-coloured scales midway between its dorsal fin and tail that could be clearly seen in the torchlight when we looked over the footbridge. Everyone in Hertford will know of the river at Hartham, but I'm guessing only a small number of anglers will be aware of the presence of a surprisingly large number of barbel and chub in the tiny shallow stream coming off the weir. For two autumns and winters Scotty and I spent countless evenings after this elusive fish.

I phoned him one cold winter's night to inform him I was going yet again to try for this fish that had refused all our attempts to put it on the bank. And although Scotty had spent the evening in intense conversation with a bottle of whisky, he wouldn't contemplate the thought of leaving me alone with the fish in case I caught it before he did. So I had to go and pick him up.

The weir was a short drive of a few minutes and as we parked-up Scotty fell out of the door and smashed his flask. I aimed him towards the river, and crossing over the bridge we settled in amongst the old sloping cemented rocks forming the opposite bank. As I made up my rod, all I could see in the darkness about twenty feet downstream of me was a ridiculous, hunched, staggering figure, muttering and swearing as he tried in vain to stab a rod rest into solid rock. After about ten minutes of this nonsense he gave up and just held the rod. Probably ten minutes after that I think we both realised Whitespot wasn't going to get out of his warm watery bed that night, so we packed up and went home.

I've no idea how many trips we made in search of that fish, but on another memorable night Scotty finally hit a bite which suggested it was a barbel. 'Suggestion' being the operative word because, at the moment of the strike, his lovely Match Aerial fell apart. One of Whitespot's little brothers of just over four pounds must have wondered what was happening on the other end as Scotty patiently, but feverishly, went about trying to put the reel back together again.

I think Fate must have had designs on killing off this reel, as I'm drawn to recall one delightfully evil night on the tiny, meandering River Lea, but further upstream on another stretch past Hertingfordbury. We were convinced, just as we are now, that the more appalling and flooded the conditions on these Hertford streams are, the better the barbel like it. Given a cloudy night and mild temperatures coupled with a stream that is flooded and still rising, barbel can sometimes be embarrassingly easy to catch.

With this in mind, following days of torrential rain, Scotty and I found ourselves parking-up on another stretch a couple of miles upriver. On opening the door of his car though, we had serious doubts on the sanity of the idea of fishing. Nevertheless, we made up our rods and strapped them on the outside of our holdalls before, in complete darkness through a wall of rain, we headed off in a kind of sideways/backwards fashion across a ploughed field. Or actually a field that was more a slop bath of mud than an actual field. When we were about half-way through this morass, in the darkness I thought I could hear a weird whirring/clicking noise. It was uncannily reminiscent of a centrepin reel slowly and relentlessly emptying. By the time we'd negotiated several trees and skirted a few bramble bushes, realisation set in. It *was* the noise of a centrepin reel slowly and relentlessly emptying. By following the line back, we eventually found the reel buried in the mud. When we finally made it to the river, which at that stage was almost in the fields, the only way Scotty could clean the mud out of the reel was by holding it underwater in the chicken soup which was doubling for river water.

Scotty's Match Aerial still lives on regardless of whatever Scotty throws at it, but every time I see it coming out of his fishing bag I wonder for how long.

(Very Handy) Andy

ONE DAY, WHILE sitting behind my lovely old cane rod, the modern plastic-topped stainless steel rod-rest it was perched on really began to irk me. It quickly got to the point when I had to do something about it. Match the rod with something just as perfectly crafted. Because of my pitiful track record of making anything myself, I decided my only recourse was to ask someone who really was a craftsman for help – my good buddy Andy Bradford.

Birdwatcher and wildlife photographer supreme, Andy is blessed with being the ultimate perfectionist in anything he touches. His fastidious

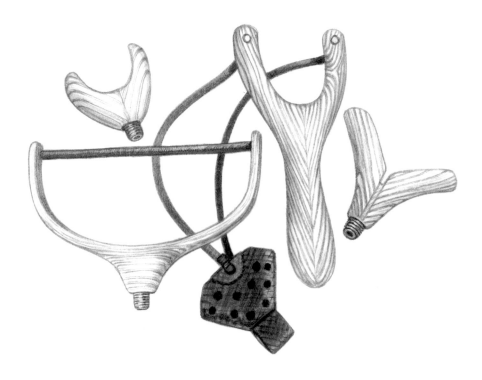

nature becomes all too apparent when you see what he is capable of when he begins to work with wood.

While Andy pondered how he was going to carve three different wooden rod-rest tops, I tried to source bamboo poles (to match my cane rod) which the rod-rests could be screwed into. Fortunately John and Brian Chapman, who took over from their father, Ron, at legendary rod makers, Chapman's of Ware, kindly gave me a bunch of reject split cane rod sections in varying lengths. These I duly handed over to a small metalworking company in Stanstead Abbotts, which added screw tops to one end and steel points to the other of the poles. I then managed (without for once making a total hash of things) to finish off the poles myself by adding whippings and then varnishing them. One evening, while Andy was midway through crafting the tops, we went over to see fishing guru, Dennis Gander, and a lovely evening was spent drinking tea, talking about fishing and photography, and poring over prototypes of Andy's fine creations.

While he was making the rod-rest tops Andy also decided to make a few catapults from the same ash wood he was using. The catapults were works of art in their own right and, as with every artist, Andy added his own personal touch – they had the look and feel of one of those old schoolboy catties jammed in the back pocket of Dennis the Menace's shorts in the *Beano*. The process of rubbing-in countless coats of teak oil took weeks in itself. Each application having to dry completely before another was added.

So now, as I sit by the corner of some forgotten pool with my old cane rod poking out from the reeds, it's a cane rod that is resting on one of Andy's perfectly coordinated rod-rests – the aesthetics of a perfect setting enhanced by Andy's consummate artistry. Whether or not any fish come to visit is, I find, increasingly immaterial – the pure pleasure of sitting by the waterside surrounded by things crafted by a dear friend is reward enough.

Our Tackle Shop

MUCH LIKE A favourite swim, I'm sure that for many of us our local favourite tackle shop is something of a personal comfort blanket. Somewhere we can retreat to and, like an Aladdin's cave, is full of everything that sparkles in our lives.

Although all tackle shops are irresistible to fishermen, there's always one above all others that we hold in the most affection. For me, and Vince, Scotty, Chad and Colin, Johnson Ross Tackle in Hoddesdon is the one.

In May 1987 Alan and Frances Johnson, together with their three sons, Anthony, Matt and Lewis, took over Ross's in Hoddesdon, shortly after Ron Ross, the previous owner died. In the years that followed, the Johnson family themselves slowly extended the shop, expanding into the two adjacent properties. Although now much larger than the original shop, and completely renovated inside, outwardly the three combined properties retain the lovely old charm from a bygone age. It says much for the Johnsons, that in tribute to Mr Ross, they retained his name alongside theirs. It is no wonder that the magic lives on.

Anthony Johnson informs me that at the turn of the century, before the days of Mr Ross, the building used to house a corn chandler and coal merchant, and before that it was the Old Harrow Inn, owned by Christies Brewery. For as long as I can remember, even before I was captivated by fishing, I always knew it as a fishing tackle shop and seed merchant. As

you walked up those familiar two brick steps and entered through the old wooden door, dear old Ron would be inside with his wife, Joy, their faces beaming, preparing to slow your day down with anything they could find to talk about. My Dad had gone to school with Mr Ross, which I thought added nicely to things.

I can picture myself now in the same scene, re-enacted every time I opened that door. I'd be inwardly yawning, standing behind two or three old women while Ron fidgeted and fussed around, measuring out bags of nuts and birdseed from old tubs behind a load of fishing rods at the back of his shop. After an age of waiting, shuffling forwards and mistakenly thinking that, as I was now finally at the front of the queue, with no one standing between Ron and myself, I'd be served. Instead, he'd pat me on the arm and say, 'Hello young Maurice, you okay for a moment?' Then he'd serve the next customer behind me – usually another old lady wanting to fatten up her bloody greenfinches.

The maggots in Ross's in those early days were a revelation. If you didn't have your own bait box, he'd drop the measured amount (a pint, two pints, whatever) together with bran, wood shavings and the odd big white chicken feather, in a brown paper bag. Then he'd hold the two corners, whirl it round a few times like a bag of sweets and hand it to you. On one memorable day during a period of a maggot shortage, my big brother Doug went in and was told by Joy that everyone was limited to just half-a-pint of maggots. Walking out the door and closing it, he stood on the step, turned round and walking back in, asked for half-a-pint of maggots. Joy said to him, 'You came in just a minute ago.' Doug looked at her and said, 'No I didn't.'

Ron had a knack of selling us (or trying to sell us) things we neither wanted or didn't need. On one particular day when my gullibility was at its height and Ron's salesmanship was at its most persuasive he had me walking out of his shop and down those steps with a set of mackerel feathers in my hand. As I had never even seen a live mackerel (I had at least that in common with those feathers), they never left my tackle box.

Over the years that I knew Ron he always showed interest in my painting, as I progressed from a young boy of twelve and into my teens when it became my career. Around the time I was seventeen, Ron kept mentioning he'd like to commission me to paint him a set of twelve original table mats, which he thought would look nice on his big oak table. I was at pains to suggest he couldn't put hot plates on original watercolours, but for some reason he wouldn't have it. Over a period of maybe two years, I finally got tired of turning down his continuing request and one day took him a framed original painting of a Redwing perched on a branch of ivy instead. He wasn't in the shop that morning so I left it there for him. I suppose the value of the painting at the time would have been around £40 or £50.

For a long while I kept missing Ron, but eventually got there when he was in the shop – as usual, standing in front of several customers. During the half-an-hour I stood there waiting he acknowledged my presence with a friendly wink, then as I neared the front, squeezed my arm and whispered, 'Hello young Maurice, I want to see you.'

It's not in my nature to presume anything or be over-ambitious in expecting anything, but I really have to admit that while I was standing there, my eyes were wandering around the jumbled shelves. Shiny new Mitchells, rods I could easily have lived with and other magnificently expensive things were pulling at me. I was spoilt for choice.

The moment everyone in the shop had been served, including the usual customers behind me in the queue, the delicious moment of reckoning arrived. At the precise moment he came to me, I idly picked up a betalight on the counter, half-an-inch long with a price tag of £1 or so on the tiny packet.

'Maurice, that painting you left was amazing. I can't thank you enough. It's wonderful, truly wonderful. What's that you have in your hand?'

Meekly, I held up the betalight. He took my hand in his, and with his other hand, gently curled my fingers shut around it. My eyes lifted, and that little glint in his eye and the smile on his face as he disappeared behind the counter, was to become a priceless memory for the sixpence jar. I miss him.

A Different Kettle ...

I SUPPOSE IT must be obvious, even to those who don't go fishing, that on some occasions those who do, merely by continually dragging a line with a hook attached through the water, will sometimes catch things other than fish.

'Hey Barry, you playing something?'

Muffled this. Mumbled that. Things going on. Splashing, a lot of splashing ...

'Yeah, blimey it's really going well.'

'You need a hand?'

'No, probably okay. Feels quite good though ...'

Scotty and I were having a three-way conversation in the rainy darkness with Barry, who was somewhere between us trying to land whatever he'd hooked. We were fishing on the little River Lea in Hertingfordbury – a favourite spot of ours, especially after dark when we were after barbel.

'This is going really well, feels very good.'

Then silence. Followed by low muttering. Then more silence.

'Barry, Barry, you okay?'

Some more indistinct mumbling. Then:

'I've caught a cow's leg.'

This was worth getting up for. Both Scotty and I went over to Barry who was now standing over his landing net in the rain, looking down at what was indeed a massive bone from a cow's leg, all two foot of it.

Unexpected as this was, the most ridiculous thing I ever put a net under was Vince's incredible folding carp.

We were fishing as always side-by-side, under the willow on the same stream but on a different stretch at Hertford Football Club. It was now dark and Vince was playing a good fish which was tearing around all over the place and definitely not in the mood to be netted. Which was just as well, because as I stood there waiting with the net, I put the torch on. Within five seconds of seeing what he'd hooked, our eyes flooded with tears of laughter and it was a wonder that it went anywhere near the net, let alone in it.

Weighing a good 11 lb 4 oz, the mirror carp, for that is exactly what it was, proceeded to fold itself in half. Exactly half way along its flank there was a vertical fold in the fish which allowed Vince, as he posed for the photos, to fold the tail completely over its face. It didn't bother the fish in the least, as apart from seemingly having no backbone for half its length, it was perfectly healthy and happy as it swam off in the torch beam, looking like a right-angled shelf bracket.

While on the subject of the unusual, I really must take my hat off to Vince, as many, many years ago (it must have been about 1969) Fate parted the clouds and allowed a little beam of sunlight to shine right down on his swim. Vince caught a burbot.

Although the story has been retold between ourselves quite a few times over the years, the actual location remains in the mists. That said, it surely must have been on the River Ouse, on one of our Greaves & Thomas Angling Society club outings that we fished as junior members. During

one of our conversations about it recently, Vince reminded me that it was about three inches long and blotchy brown in colour. And in answer to my question yet again as to whether it could have been a loach and not a burbot, he remembered it as having long continuous dorsal and anal fins – which *undoubtedly* confirms it as being a small burbot ... and Vince as being something I'd rather not mention.

While the Cat's Away

IT'S COMFORTING TO know that ridiculous things can happen to our little band even without me being there. I was beginning to think my aura and ability to attract the absurd was the reason stupid things happened to us, but it's nice to know they're fully capable of attracting quirkiness on their own.

Like the day at Walthamstow Reservoir on one of Steve's trips when, as he was quietly sitting there waiting for his next fish, a squirrel fell out of the large overhanging willow just above his head. Dropping twenty feet straight into the water, it swam to the bank, shook itself and ran back up the tree.

Or when Scotty packed the car the night before an early morning start on a grayling fishing trip with Barry and Dave. The idea was that it would save him a lot of bother before he set off. Everything went to plan except for his inability to understand the word 'securely' when closing the lid on his bait bucket. This led to the mass exodus of nearly a gallon-and-a-half of maggots into every nook and cranny of his car. Little did he realise the amount of bother the maggots would cause his wife, Liz, a few months later when he was away for a week working in Madrid. The weather turning hot, the maggots began hatching out, setting off the car alarm.

Investigating, Liz opened the door and was enveloped by a cyclone of thousands of hungry flies. They continued to hatch for about a month and eventually flattened the car battery, the alarm going off all the time. If that wasn't bad enough, tired of the endless fly hatch, Liz eventually emptied a can of fly spray inside the car. This, while killing everything that crawled, hatched or lived in the car, unfortunately led to a horrific rotting and decomposing smell that haunted the car for a good year or two.

I always smile when Vince reminds me of the day, many years ago, when he and a mutual fishing buddy of ours, Steve Lotcho, drove all the way up to Norfolk for a day's roach fishing. On arrival they discovered they'd left all the bait at home, so they sat in the car, ate their sandwiches and came back.

Regarding the absurd, I really must take my hat off to Vince again who was in France for a week, happily fishing for carp with his son, George. A lovely hot sunny day, Vince was sitting back in his chair relaxing with his legs stretched out, feet crossed. While chatting away with George, he pointed out a hapless fly that had aimlessly landed on the tip of one of his trainers. For reasons best known to George, he decided to throw a rock at it, smashing into Vince's toe. It caused the nail to go completely black, then fall off. Like father like son I suppose.

One morning's fishing I'm glad I missed out on was the occasion when Scotty made an early morning start after tench at Heartbreak Lake in Nazeing. His dawn arrival coincided with the tench in most co-operative mood, and with a storm closing in on him, two or three hit the net. He was fishing the spot we referred to as the silver birch swim. (Memory fails both of us as to where the silver birch actually stood, but for the sake of this little story it doesn't really matter.) The lightning bolt, which speared out of nowhere and hit the water just off the end of his rod, sent him flying off his chair. Not wishing to disprove the old story about lightning never striking the same spot twice and not wanting to tempt the next into landing ten feet nearer, he quickly packed his gear. Then swathed in the acrid stench of burning sulphur he left his swim full of fried tench, and went home.

M.J.PLEDGER.

IN THE SWIM

I came to realise at a very early age that I have an affinity with the absurd.

The Bermuda Triangle, Kempston

SITUATED JUST OUTSIDE Kempston, and apparently within the Bermuda Triangle, lies our club section of the River Ouse – Box End Farm. For reasons attributable to the geography around Kempston, local climatic conditions, ley lines and who knows what else, anytime we even think about fishing the place or going anywhere near it, 'things' happen.

From the very first moment Abbey Cross Angling Society gained the fishing rights, and one of the members, Pete Arnold, told us of the unbelievable fish we could expect, we knew it was somewhere we just had to visit. His description of a lovely wide natural river with medium flow, flanked by overhanging trees on the far bank and extensive beds of reeds on ours, was absolutely spot on. Pete's directions to get there though, with convoluted left turns, right turns (which may or may not have existed), T-junctions which he may have imagined in his dreams or from trips to India were, most decidedly, not spot on.

Our first three or four trips were mainly spent taking in the delights of the outlying areas of Bedfordshire. Subsequent careful questioning of Pete, in the vain hope of securing a few short cuts, got us no closer to finding the place. The first time we actually set foot on the bank I should have realised we were up against things we had no control over, like the fact that the river was flowing the wrong way. No matter how many times we went, nothing I could do would change this, so I just had to live with it. The only help I ever got with this river-flowing-the-wrong-way thing, was on the day we arrived to find the place unfishable and so choked with cabbages and lilies, it really didn't matter which way it was flowing, because it wasn't.

Then, for some reason, the mere suggestion of planning a trip to Box End would have every anti-cyclone, depression, storm system and monsoon heading over to Kempston in defiance of weather reports, which promised a series of perfect days. And like a big cooking pot in the sky, the systems would mix and swirl into a maelstrom just waiting for us to arrive.

As we normally like to quivertip at Box End, naturally the weather system favoured by the gods was wind … and rain. Yes, wind and rain were good. Gale force and torrential, even better. Naturally the days either side of the one on which we'd chosen to fish were full of buttercups and corn poppies, warbling skylarks and fluttery butterflies.

The entrance to Box End Farm (when we eventually found it) was off the aptly-named Cemetery Road, through a five-barred gate alongside an equestrian farm. After a hundred yards, the gravel track turned abruptly right, bordered a few trees, then left across a big, wide-open field. The track flanked a drainage ditch and carried on for two hundred yards until it reached the river. A fish hook turn at the end, over the ditch and a park-up for the day next to an enormous grassy mound. The swims we generally fished were near the car.

Instructions from Pete were written, I'm guessing, while he was reading from his upside-down backstreets-of-Bengal snakes-and-ladders map, and always included the following: 'Drive down to the river, then you can follow the bank all the way down in the car and park behind your swim'.

'All the way down' was several hundred yards along the rutted edge of a ploughed field, that when wet (which it always was), looked something like a giant rice paddy.

But on that lovely, crisp, frosty, morning when Vince and I arrived in his new car, all boded well. Through the gate, along a way, turn right, then left, and across the nice crunchy gravelly field, make a fish hook turn over the ditch and park up by the mound. As we sat in our crispy-crunchy swims tackling up, everything was so strangely wonderful and perfect, we began to think the gods of wind and rain had got the date wrong, and were instead out over the Atlantic somewhere sinking a few trawlers. I swear even the sun shone for a little while. I even caught several tiny roach and when I looked a few yards downstream at Vince, he was busy with a couple of small chub.

Then, bored with the trawlers, the gods came back, and on finding the pair of us obviously much too happy with how the day was going, swirled up a few menacing black clouds, unzipped the lot and finished our day off in style.

It rained and rained and rained. Then it rained some more. It was still raining when we slammed the doors on Vince's car and made to drive off. *Made to* drive off is all we did. No amount of shoving, pushing, leaning, swearing or anything made the slightest difference. The car slewed around and dug itself in, the back wheels spinning like manic Catherine wheels in a mud bath. Eventually though, after shoving several forests of branches under the wheels, I watched as Vince slithered off, crablike, in palls of smoke towards the farm that was just visible in the rain-sodden distance. By a miracle he eventually got there, and I hopped in and we drove off to a car wash in Kempston. Even after the car went through it, we still needed to stop off later at a jet wash in Bengeo where Vince blasted the remaining mud out of it. As we drove off, the piles of mud we left on the forecourt would have filled several buckets.

Sometimes though, despite the efforts of the gods, our persistence in fishing in conditions most people would be checking their insurance policies for flood damage clauses, paid off. Our next trip was such a day. The river was almost breaking into the fields, but our favourite swims near the car offered a little respite from the wind and the torrential rain for once held off. As usual I was using a light quivertip and spent a few hours happily catching some small roach. Downstream of me by a few yards sat Vince.

Judging by the type of bites he was missing, it was obvious he'd attracted a few chub around him with the large block-end feeder and maggots he was using. In between striking thin air, he connected with two or three of a couple of pounds.

The river was carrying an extra two foot of water and thanks to heavy rain during the week the surroundings looked pretty muddy and bleak. Vince's rod went over again and, as his line cut through the swirling grey water, this time it wasn't heading towards our bank. (The chub at Box End always dived under the masses of dead reeds tangled against the bank, but this one had no intention at all of coming anywhere near us.)

'I think I might need a hand with this one.'

I reeled in and slithered over to Vince who was now on his feet and trying to stand upright without falling in. I can only guess that whatever Vince was attached to was by now only showing mild irritation as to what was holding up its afternoon, if it knew it was hooked at all. Connected only by 4 lb line and a piddling size 14 spade-end hook, Vince was in no position to do anything other than hold on, not fall in, and ignore my inane comments as I stood beside him with the landing net.

After about ten minutes of just watching his line cut through the irresistible flow, we were both wondering what was below. With every passing minute, the possibilities of what would eventually rise up in the water tangled our minds. Then, for a brief second, it allowed itself to be brought to the surface, where it rolled momentarily then powered off down again to the bottom.

With that fleeting glimpse of a broad, almost greyish-white flank, and strangely angular pointed fin, we both began to think Vince had attached himself to some impossible kind of sea fish. Or maybe some weirdly exotic species that someone had tired of and released years before, and which had grown up unseen and unmolested amongst the shoals of chub.

We had to wait another long five minutes more though as the fish (was it a fish?) resumed its position, holding over the gravels in the relentless current underneath Vince's hooped rod. And then the fish finally relented and, as all good barbel do when they are completely spent, allowed itself to be drawn across the surface to where I waited for it to quietly drift back into the net.

Truly one of those special sixpence jar moments. Unforgettable, and as the scales were lifted, the hand on the dial began to whizz round. Most of the fish was still lying on the bank as the marker passed ten pounds, and when it finally slowed down and gave up, we both realised that this was the king of barbel at an unbelievable thirteen pounds.

Gently released to resume its afternoon's travels, we both admitted that the brief glimpse we had of its flank as it turned over had completely fooled us. Had the hook pulled at that precise moment I honestly think we'd still be wondering quite what Vince had hooked that grey winter's day a few years ago.

Absurd

I CAME TO realise at a very early age that I have an affinity with the absurd.

Whether or not I have an ability to unknowingly create absurdity from nothing, or it unerringly comes to find me while I'm fishing, I don't know. But there it is. Nothing I can do about it even if I wanted to. So I just sit back and enjoy the ride. Or not enjoy it as the case may be.

Like the day I walked up to Barbara Newton's front door at the Lock House at King's Weir and stuck my right hand through her letter box to place a £2 coin for the car park on to the ledge inside. What I actually did was to shove the coin straight into the slavering mouth of a massive white dog that usually was quite happy to see me. On this particular day though it wasn't too impressed with the hand that shoved a coin into its mouth, so it sunk its teeth into it and tried to rip it off my wrist. Snarling and shaking its head like a demented crocodile it made a pretty good job of it. The one-

handed drive home, loss of blood, hospital trip and tetanus jab certainly took my mind off missing the day's fishing.

King's Weir wasn't quite finished with me though as another absurd event happened soon after my hand had healed. I was back in Barbara's garden, loading up my tackle and walking over to Swim Three West, directly in front of her house. As I passed Swim Five, I paused and stood behind two anglers sitting side by side with their backs to me. Precisely at that moment, a huge cormorant surfaced right between their two rods about three yards out and, with the raucous chaotic tidal wave only a panicking cormorant can create, it exploded into running flight. One of the anglers turned to the other, calmly pointed at what was once their swim and said, 'That was a great crested grebe.'

Enjoying my early morning lesson in alternative ornithology I shouldered my tackle once again and walked over to Three West where I tackled up and started fishing. I'd only been there about an hour when I noticed a young angler crossing over the weir bridge, entering the gate on the other side of the pool and walking over to a man who was already happily fishing with his little son aged about four. (They were in my favourite swim, Three East, 'The Beach'.)

I didn't pay too much attention but after a good five minutes, the young guy crossed back over the bridge having left the man, who was now shaking his head, to carry on fishing. Obviously, whatever he wanted, the young guy had found no joy so he came to try me.

'Excuse me mate, you couldn't help me out could you?'

I turned to look at him, standing somewhat forlorn behind me with a white rag wrapped around one hand.

'What's happened?'

'Er, I've got a big hook shoved into my finger. It's really in deep. It's not coming out. I can't drive. Can you take me to the hospital?'

After about ten minutes of intense conversation, mostly about which hospital would be the best to go to, I reluctantly decided that I'd put my Good Samaritan hat on, forego my day's fishing and help out the poor guy. As he walked off we agreed that I'd meet him back at the car park after I'd packed all my tackle away. As I made my way back to the car, I passed the two would-be ornithologists in Swim Five again, noticing that one of them had packed up while the other one fished on. As they said their goodbyes, I realised that the one who had packed up was the guy with the hook embedded in his finger. Kicking my slow uptake into gear, I asked him who the other angler was, he said:

'Oh, he's my uncle. We came in the same car, but he doesn't want me to ruin his day's fishing.'

At which point I turned around, walked back to my swim and tackled up again. Eventually I heard the uncle's car drive off, and towards the end of the day they returned, after having toured all the various hospitals that they, with their combined IQs of around five, could find.

Still with his hand wrapped in the same, now slightly less-white rag, the young guy came over to tell me what had happened. Apparently they'd spent the afternoon waiting around several hospitals, but none of them would remove the hook without him staying in for a bit, so they'd returned to the weir so his uncle could get a few last casts in.

Then there was the minor episode of the swimming lessons on the River Stort at Sawbridgeworth. Scotty and I were fishing but not much was happening. I yawned, stretched, got up out of my chair and ambled off to look for him somewhere upstream. At various points along the stretch, someone had built some long, narrow stages reaching out into the deeper water, and it was on the end of one of these that I found him. Not standing on the edge, but clambering out of the water. Or, rather, trying to.

In between coughing and choking, I think he was trying to laugh as I helped drag him out. It'd been raining and the stage was wet and slippery. Apparently he'd been standing on the extreme edge when a small pike of around three pounds launched itself at his bait, right under his feet. It was fifty/fifty who was the most surprised – him or the pike – but I'm guessing it was Scotty as the explosion of spray at his feet caused him to slip and fall in with it.

I suppose I really shouldn't have laughed, as a short while later, this time on a day which was boot-deep with snow, Scott's little guardian angelfish waved her little wand at me.

I'd just caught a pike of about five pounds and thought it nice enough to have a photo taken of me with it. Scotty duly obliged and I turned round to face the stream, pike in hand, leaned over to gently release it, and just kept going. In the split second when I realised what was to come, I tucked my head into my belt and somehow completely spun over, and like something I can only describe as a spinning crayfish, went straight in with the pike. Or a half-pike with a twist, with a pike, you could say.

Later, perhaps even more absurd, was the day of the Walthamstow gate – the big, heavy, solid iron, automatically rising and lowering iron bar of a gate that stretches across the entrance of Walthamstow Reservoirs in Tottenham. It's a gate so massive that I'm convinced it spent its early years holding back the Titanic in the shipyard. Anyone fishing the reservoirs will know it. This is a gate with a mind of its own. You never really know whether it's going to automatically lift or not when you approach it, although in the mornings when there's a lot going on, it usually does. In the afternoons though, when there isn't too much happening, it doesn't.

On this particular late afternoon as Scotty and I were returning from yet another fruitless (for me) day's fishing on Reservoir No.1 we approached the great beast of ironmongery, the gate of hell. I was in front and as I walked up to the thing with my fishing tackle on a trolley, I said:

'Don't worry, it never opens this time of the day.'

To be honest, I only got about half of it said, when the gate took to the air, shooting up right under my nose and nearly taking my head off. When I came round and re-assured Scotty I was more or less okay, my nose had swollen to the size of something that normally grows on the side of a tree. A tree that had been previously struck by a meteorite.

Jonah and the Bream

IT'S FUNNY HOW a little thread can follow you throughout your life, winding its way as you go, and as you look back over your shoulder you realise that even after many years there it is still unbroken.

One particular thread began on 10 October, 1971, on one of my early fishing trips with my old friend Steve Tibble, and has followed me throughout my life. As I sit here and write more than forty years later, I have no doubt that it will continue to unravel endlessly into the future. It concerns bream or, rather, their unnerving ability to steer clear of me particularly when Steve is around. That's not to say that I've never caught a bream when Steve has been around – there was a glorious 7 lb 6 oz specimen I caught at the North Met the same night Steve had one of 7 lb 10 oz. Mistakenly I foolishly imagined this would be just the beginning of my long succession of big bream.

Anyway let's wind the clock back to that particular day. Picture us sitting side-by-side on one of the last swims along King's Weir where Steve

M.F.PLEDGER.

and I were casting lobworms over to an overhanging willow on the other bank. I'd caught a chub of three pounds and Steve a barbel of a pound. As I wanted to catch a barbel and Steve a chub, we swapped over, and again I had a chub and Steve a barbel. This carried on for a while and no amount of swapping would get me a barbel, just more chub.

As our next trip together was not after barbel but bream, this didn't worry me too much. All I wanted to do was catch a bream one ounce heavier than 7 lb 6 oz. During one of the worst storms that we've ever fished in the bream I hooked from the depths of Steve's swim would, I imagine, have dwarfed it. Imagining it was as near as I got though, as it circled around in the torchlight on the surface waiting to be netted and attached to what I thought was one of the strongest hooks in my box. The bream thought otherwise and snapped it off at the bend. Before it melted into the darkness in the torrential rain it let us watch it for a few seconds in the beam just off the landing net, which I thought was a nice touch.

During the following years I've run it close a few times but never while I was fishing with Steve. And anyway, every time I got anywhere near actually landing a bigger one, something happened and it fell off. I even lassoed one while wobbling sprats one cold winter's day and foul-hooked another when I cast into a shoal of spawning fish. Both were heavier than my 7 lb 6 oz North Met bream but were landed unfairly. An absolutely huge bream I hooked at Rye Meads on the stroke of midnight years later, waved its tail at me in the moonlight before the hook pulled out. A sparkling little memory.

The thread was obviously still attached when, in September 2009, Steve and I began to share our fishing trips on one particular wooden stage in No. 1 Reservoir on the Walthamstow complex in Tottenham.

Several times during the first few weeks of the new season Steve and I found ourselves perched on the end of the stage, casting four identical baits side-by-side in a line in our favourite spot. Quite why it's my favourite spot I have no idea because I've yet to catch anything from it remotely resembling a bream. On any one trip we continually swap sides – the idea still that by doing so would give me some kind of chance to catch a bream. It doesn't. Steve will catch three or four while I sit there looking through my indicators watching the daphnia bloom. We change sides again. It gives Steve a few moments respite before he continues to add to his catch from my side, bless him. The only difference being it gives the clouds of daphnia a chance to settle down a little while he's not pulling fish through them.

Recounting every bream Steve has caught, and the number of times we swapped sides, would serve only to bore you with the continuing impossibility of me ever breaking the thread. As I write, his tally of bream up to an incredible 12 lb 6 oz numbers fifty-one fish over eight pounds. My tally for fish over 7 lb 6 oz is … zero.

Nothing surprises me any more in my quest to catch a bream over the weight of that early North Met fish. However, in a strange way I think if I ever did it would probably mean less to me than that one. In any case, it's never going to happen.

The moral of the story, I think, is 'don't swap swims with Jonah' or in this case Steve.

Two Worlds Meet

AS I WEND my solitary way around the margins of the lake I come to the course of the old stream and follow it. There are still faint signs of the winding bends and the gravelly shallows just where they used to be many years ago before the fields were flooded. These bends and shallows hold interest for me and for many of my cousins. For along the old course the vegetation following its path differs slightly from the contours and areas surrounding it. Bullrushes seem to like the areas of gravel and in turn they attract the perch, although I know they cannot resist investigating when one of the willows topples into the water. For a while at least, they like to frequent the area, cruising through the branches and picking at drowned insects within the old moss and lichens.

There are also many roach in the lake and no small number of chub. I always remember seeing them swimming alongside the shoals of roach, while the larger ones tend to drift off in twos and threes and bask in the shallow water alongside the bleached dead branches and twigs of the old drowned bushes. There are many areas like this surrounding the edges of the lake. An odd carp cruises through every now and then, and although they also keep pretty much to themselves, they sometimes come and investigate if a shoal of roach have found food. They never hang around too long and after a few minutes they just drift off through the weeds while the little fish return to their pickings.

In one corner of the lake, in a lovely forgotten reedy bay, there is a nice bed of old swan mussels half-buried in the silt. They never seem to be doing much, but a little while ago I was attracted to some small movements in the area, but it was only a gathering of water scorpions clambering all over the mussels. I watched for a bit, but after a while I left them to it and continued on my way around the edges of the lake.

The water level in the lake frequently rises, and within a very short time the surrounding area becomes inundated, sometimes to the extent that other ponds close-by merge into one huge lake. At times like this the pike like to lie quietly in the now underwater long grass, but for the moment the levels are low and they've retreated back down to the dark shadowy corners once again.

Three hours from now the sun will rise, and only then will the upper layers of water begin to warm as shards of gold burn off the mist and dance through the ripples over the bar. For now the water is cool but not excessively so. The night was calm and uneventful, and as I make my way along the route I have travelled for many years I sense movement below me and pause to look. The water here is shallow. I carry on a little way over the bar into deeper water to where I reach the edge of a spit where there's a small patch of weeds under some young willows. It is here that I notice some little grubs moving in the silt. I investigate and begin my meal, picking at the succulent offerings before me. Above me I notice the glow of a strange subdued light, it worries me, but the food is irresistible …

I'm on one of the 'new' lakes at Rye Meads. In the darkness of early morning the glow of the small betalight in the top of my float is strangely hypnotic, comforting almost. In the quiet solitude before an early dawn the dim light gives me some kind of focus. It had been a long walk from the car in the dark, but the path was familiar. I'd followed the course of the stream which bordered the lakes, remembering the times years ago when I watched birds in the field with Dad and fished the stream with Chad and Vince before it got 'moved' to one side to accommodate the new landscape. It amazes me how the level of the stream can rise so much in times of flooding – completely covering the path and turning the whole area into one huge lake. Luckily the start of the season had coincided with it being very low and, as I reached the end lake, I turned left and made my way along to a heavily wooded area of young sapling willows. These grew in profusion on a spit of marshy land which jutted out onto the lake, like an island almost. Looking like a mangrove swamp in the daylight, thirty yards of negotiating it in the dark with all my tackle, was like being lost in one. After a few detours I finally made it on to the very edge of the island and leaning my chair

against the last tree amongst the reeds, I was now precariously balanced with the water at my feet.

Within minutes I was fishing, my little betalight nicely half-cocked about three feet off my rod tip. The bait, a couple of maggots wriggling in the silt five feet below on the edge of a little patch of amphibious bistort.

I had no way of knowing but our worlds were about to collide.

A gentle waft of the betalight was enough to alert me that something was around my bait. Another waver of my float … nothing really deliberate, but just enough to keep my hands on the corks. A few more seconds of nothing … a tiny dip … then relaxing into the perfect lift bite. I probably struck before it fell flat. My rod was in a full curve before the fish had even gone a couple of yards. Already I was praying for the small hook to hold as it drove off towards the end of the bar twenty yards out in the darkness. I knew the area well and there were no obstructions to worry about except perhaps a small patch of lilies away off at the end of the bar. My only fear was that the hook would pull out – a thought that I really didn't need at that particular moment.

On its first irresistible run, the fish made the bar easily. It could have just as easily travelled further into the lilies, but for some reason it turned, and thankfully headed back my way. The fish stayed deep, all the way to my feet where it circled and bore down into the silt amongst the weed where it had been feeding. Preparing my landing net, I shortened the line between us as I watched the long leaves and stems of the bistort curl and sway like drunken snakes beneath the glow of the betalight. I knew that, if Fate was looking the other way, within a few moments I would be drawing my fish over the net. Winding the remaining few turns of line on my Aerial I sensed it was ready and glided it into the mesh.

I quickly prepared a few things and drew the fish toward me. In the dim glow of my torch I could see the face of a lovely tench within the folds of netting. Carefully removing the small hook I placed the tench in a weighing sling and began to lift. And lift and lift and lift. Incredibly the needle had passed seven pounds and the fish was still flat in the water's edge. I went through the motions three times before I allowed the needle to come to rest. I could not believe what I was seeing. I still could not believe it even when I looked away and looked again. Before I could even give my mind a chance to think again, I bit my line and packed away all my tackle. I left the tench comfortably in the keep net hidden away from view, made sure it was okay and ran back to the car. I left all my tackle at home and drove round to Mum and Dad's. It was a Sunday morning and only just getting light, probably somewhere around four o'clock. Unlocking the door and saying a quiet hello to Rusty, their dog, I crept upstairs to where they were both asleep. Explaining things to Dad, he immediately got dressed and he, Rusty and I returned to the lake.

In daylight the tench looked even more impressive. We weighed it again – 9 lb exactly. Photos taken, we gently released it back to its home where it drifted off back to the bar.

The walk back to the car was made even more memorable as we watched a fox stalk some Canada geese asleep on the bank. At some point they sensed it creeping up on them and hopped into the lake and paddled off, adjusting a few feathers. This was all thirty years ago now and I fondly remember it was the second time Dad had come to my rescue photographing my best tench. Another sixpence dropped in the jar.

FISHING TACKLE

*Today I'll be showing you the most important item of fishing tackle you'll
ever need.*

Plummeting Earthwards ...

JACK HARGREAVES AND *Out Of Town*. It was sometime in the mid-
1960s, Vince and I had spent all week since the previous episode waiting,
counting the days, and now here we were, sitting in front of the old black
and white television set, completely transfixed, hoping he wouldn't be
talking about horses again. There he sat in his old shed and said: 'Today I'll
be showing you the most important item of fishing tackle you'll ever need.'

If Vince's bottom jaw wasn't laying on the carpet in front of us, mine
certainly was. Out of our skins in anticipation, we waited until Jack got
some other shed stuff out of the way, almost paralysed by the thought of
what it could be. Was it perhaps a magic rod I just had to get Mum and Dad
to buy for me? An even more magical reel? Or line that actually attracted
fish? Whatever it was, I needed one. I would have loved to have seen the
quizzical look on my own face as Jack, now out of his shed and sitting
amongst some reeds at the riverside, attached a plummet to his hook and
lowered it into the water. My heaving chest, deflating by the second as Jack
continued, 'Yes, the most important piece of tackle you'll ever need is a
plummet. I've had mine for thirty years and wouldn't go fishing without it.'

Faster than it took for Jack's film editor to splice the shed sequence to the
riverbank sequence, we were at Ross's, our local tackle shop in Hoddesdon,
and soon after sitting side-by-side in our own little patch of reeds by the
waterside. I was now looking at the plummet in my hand – puzzled.

Hanging 'the most important item of tackle I'll ever need' through the

bend of my hook, I lowered it in the water in front of me and lifted it out. Only it didn't lift out. It fell off. Either I was completely stupid, or Jack was the most supremely efficient angler in history – if only for managing to keep his plummet for thirty years. I immediately thought about how I was going to hide how supremely inefficient I was from Vince, rather than tell him. The thought lasted about as long as my plummet, as Vince had just been sitting there watching me all the while.

Along with our inseparable mate Richard Clayden (always known as Chad), we played conkers and marbles. We also flicked Brooke Bond PG Tips cards against the school wall and, if luck was going my way, if any of mine landed on one of the others gathering on the ground by the wall in front of us, I kept the lot. If my luck was out, they did. Maybe they flicked better than me, but I was always careful not to use any of my freshwater fish collection, much preferring to lose my bird cards painted by C. F. Tunnicliffe, however much I prized them. The fish cards, painted by Ernest Petts, were so evocative of everything that was fishing to kids of twelve-years-old, that every fish we wanted to catch had to look like one of those paintings. My favourite of his was of a chub rising up in some fast water – but not one of the many hundreds of chub I've caught in these intervening years have looked as good as that one. Or maybe I've been catching dace all these years – all up to 7 lb 6 oz. Yes, that's what it must be.

We watched *Lost in Space*. To my mind, and I think without doubt to every sane thinking person in the whole world, that old series was the best thing ever shown on television, even to this day. And in any case, I had the most impossible crush on Penny Robinson – not that I ever let on to the others.

It was also at this time, that during a visit to the school by the school doctor, it was discovered I was abysmally red-green colour blind. It was something we all had a lot of fun with over the years, and the reason why all the tips on my floats are bright yellow. My fishing pals insistence on using only red-tipped floats – ones I can't bloody see, mirrored against any amount of reflected leafy vegetation – is probably because they don't want me to notice how many bites they aren't getting.

Along with maths, Chad was better at woodwork than either Vince or I. He decided to make some floats. And I suppose because of this, I decided to give it a try too.

I can picture myself now, intent as any Swiss cuckoo clock maker, hunched over the vice attached to the bench in Dad's shed, feverishly cutting, chiselling and filing away at nothing less than masterpieces of fishing art. With the benefit of hindsight, my time would probably have been better spent trying to find a live Smurf. For some vague reason, I decided on (and I use the term loosely) *perfecting* half-a-dozen narrow-stemmed, yellow-tipped, balsa wood antenna floats. An even more vague reason prompted me to paint the best one – which took far, far, longer to make than the others – with a red tip. Several coats of varnish and a hell of a long time later, they were finished.

I remember the date and place of their baptism well – 28 November, 1971, Kings Weir along the River Lea, a few hundred yards down from the pool. God knows why we tried upstream of a large, overhanging, willow tree as the water, hurtling through possibly three feet above normal and the colour of grey paint, suggested we should really sit below it. So this is where we ended up, sheltering downstream of the tree with a short section of completely dead water at our feet of about twelve feet long and three feet wide. Further out, looking through the rain, weed, branches and the odd bush floated by in the raging torrent in which we decided to run the trial. At the ready was my match rod, Mitchell 314, 2 lb line, red-tipped Swiss cuckoo clock maker's example of excellence, dust shot, size 16 hook, and one maggot. I swung it out. I'm sure the law of physics, added to the law of my own inability to doing anything right, was the reason why immediately my masterpiece of a float, sunk just as effortlessly as if I'd tied an anvil to it. So I cut it off and used something I'd bought from Ross's instead.

Seeing something of its potential though, or perhaps out of pity for me and all my efforts of making it, Vince leant over, took the accursed thing out of my tackle box, and decided to give it the baptism it deserved. The design of the float, such as it was (as it certainly had nothing else going for it), decreed it needed no shot whatsoever. Shotted, it cocked and disappeared immediately, but without the dust shot added, it lifted up just enough for the very tip of it to almost break through the surface film – just enough for an ant to cling to. Which, truth be told, would probably have made it sink again. First drop in, the dimple disappeared. Vince struck. It was a chub; he lost it. Second cast … actually this could get very laboured … six casts, six lost chub. The float was unceremoniously dumped back in the box, and never saw the light of day again. I'd like to think it still exists somewhere (as what I don't know) but the memory of it and Vince's six lost chub was certainly worth a couple of hours of my time making the pointless thing.

... and Hitting the Ground

JUST BEFORE THE great float trial took place (and Vince's lost chub record), we were on the tiny little stream which comes off the Lea about eighty yards above King's Weir. It begins its life as a miniature weir pool, then meanders along a little way before branching off again, flanking the large lake which sits alongside the River Lea. It was one of our favourite haunts. We named it Kip's Stream – though the reason why is lost in the mists of time.

Forty years later, the tiny weir is still there, as is the little meandering stream feeding into King's Weir pool, but the stretch that branched off unfortunately is now gone. The three of us loved that little stream. Dead straight, with barely any flow and, at its deepest, maybe two-and-a-half-feet, once we'd tucked in below the skyline and held our match rods across the water, the tips would almost be touching the vegetation on the other side. It was small stream fishing at its very, very best – the largest dace we caught was maybe a shade under four ounces, with the largest chub going to Vince at about fourteen ounces.

One memory (and not such a really wonderful one) that does stand out more than the others, was the event of 17 October, 1971. About ten minutes before we were due to pack up we got (as always) a bit silly. To set the scene: earlier during the day I'd broken a rod rest followed by Chad writing off two of his. It really was one of those days. Then Chad, after having distanced himself from his float by about fifteen yards (and his common sense by about fifteen miles) announced to Vince and myself, that he was going to do a 'match strike'.

So that's exactly what he did. I will never forget the sight of his dad's lovely traditional 13 ft Spanish reed match rod with a split cane tip and the beautiful arc it made in response to Chad's Herculean match strike. Nor will I ever forget the sounds the lovely traditional 13 ft Spanish reed match rod made during the beautiful arc – the mighty 'whoosh' as it was swept upwards – the rifle shot crack as it broke neatly in half.

Schemes and Gadgets, Mr Bond

I COULD ONLY have been about ten-years-old.

I was with Mum and Dad and they'd taken me to visit Mum's uncle, Zio Fidenzio at his old house in Bologna. I remember sitting at an old wooden table in his dimly lit kitchen, the silhouetted shapes of the family casting shadows against the claustrophobic stone walls as they moved around making coffee and talking grown-up stuff. Great-uncle Fidenzio, the only time I ever saw him, turned away from the shadows and placed an old box on the table in front of me. His tackle box. Great-uncle Fidenzio was a fellow fisherman.

He was a kindly, learned old soul, well into his seventies, and although he didn't let on to me, he probably knew he wouldn't be seeing us again. He had learned of my interest in fishing and as he talked to me about secretive fishy things, he first brought out a box of polenta – Italian ground maize flour. Bright yellow in colour, when prepared and cooked it makes a kind of hot dish a bit like mashed potato. However if you simply added water to it and mix, it makes a superb paste for fishing.

Then he produced a little invention of his own and said I could have it. Outwardly looking like a red and white pike bung he proudly exclaimed it to be his 'self-striking float', and showed me how the ingenious device worked. The line was threaded down the centre of the float through an intricate narrow metal tube. The float could now be set at the desired depth by the simple means of lightly hitching up the line at the base of the tube. When pulled gently a tiny little lever inside the tube would raise up and catch across it thereby trapping the line. Down below would be the baited hook, and when this was taken by a fish the slight pull would cause the device to snap back up, sharply tugging the line an inch and setting the hook.

Finally, just before we went, Great-uncle Fidenzio brought out another box. Its contents, he said, were top secret. It was tightly sealed, but leaking out of it was a strange, somewhat pungent smell which, come to think of

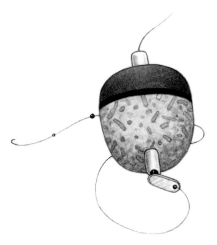

it, pervaded his entire kitchen. He told me that inside the box was a bait so powerful that there was no fish living that could resist it. And then he pressed it into my hands …

Sadly, Great-uncle Fidenzio passed away before we could see him again but I carried his float in my tackle box for quite a few years afterwards. I hardly used it though, mainly through my own stupidity – because it had the appearance of a pike bung, I thought it could only be used for pike fishing. The only time I tried it out was with a sprat suspended beneath it. Unfortunately the weight of the sprat was enough to set off the delicate mechanism every time I cast it out. Of course he'd designed it with small fish in mind, and because I never used it in this way, I never used it correctly. Somewhere along the way it went missing and to this day I regret not keeping it safely at home.

I guess somewhere along the line Great-uncle Fidenzio's inventive genes, or at least an appreciation of inventiveness, must have weakly (very weakly) passed through my mother's family to me. However, left to my own devices and under no-one's guidance, I cannot truthfully say any of my schemes or inventions ever came to very much. Here though are a few examples:

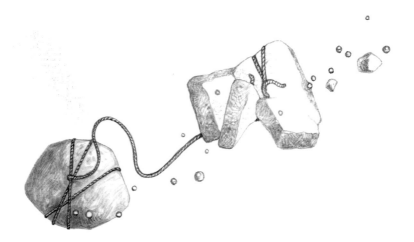

Take the *Richard Walker Rudd Attractor*. I was eleven. The fishing book I kept borrowing from the school library had a neat little drawing in the rudd chapter of a floating piece of dried bread, anchored in one spot by a length of line and a stone. This simply fiendish and sneaky method for attracting rudd was one of Dick Walker's own ideas, and as such couldn't possibly fail.

The first day I decided to give it an airing was on the Conkers stretch of the River Lea in Nazeing, opposite a row of houseboats. I was fishing the river for the first time with a bunch of mates in our class, and while no one was looking, I reached into my bag for the slice of bread I'd previously attached via three feet of string to a brick. I think you could confidently say my version of the *Richard Walker Rudd Attractor* worked like a dream. Until the moment it hit the water that is – my slice of bread floating for about three seconds before it was dragged under permanently.

Then there was my brother Doug's tench rake, his pride and joy – although I've never understood why. It was essentially a big lump of hollowed-out wood with molten lead poured inside and a row of six inch nails hammered

90

through it. Foolishly allowing me to borrow it, as I hurled it out into my tench swim at the North Met that warm sunny afternoon, the pathetically thin parcel string I'd attached it to parted like a cobweb. Again, a resounding success. On a more positive note, forty-two years later I still know where it is.

Then fly-tying. Hours on end spent chopping up my feather collection and tying various bits of anything that looked pretty to old bronze hooks was, I'd say, even less of a success. Nothing was immune to my handiwork – pheasant feathers, jay feathers, starling feathers, tied one at a time; or pheasant feathers, jay feathers, starling feathers tied all mixed together. They lived in a Rowntree's Blackcurrant Pastilles tin for years and were so forgettable that I can't even remember when I lost them or the tin.

I cannot even begin to tell you the hours I spent making pike plugs. My best one I actually did cast once but even I was embarrassed when it swam back towards me sideways. It was made out of a piece of old rabbit skin I'd sewed onto two wooden duffle coat toggles, with a long dangly furry tail hanging out the back. It was supposed to look like a swimming rat. Whether or not it would have done so on subsequent casts I wouldn't know. It never got the chance.

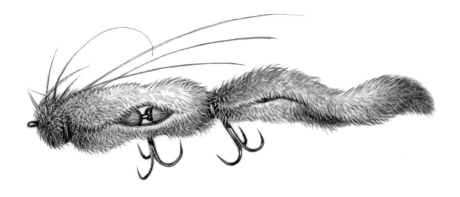

Dad's 35mm film canisters were turned into swim-feeders in front of our open fire with holes melted into the sides with a red-hot poker. I used these swim-feeders as an alternative to the ones made out of Mum's hair curlers. These almost worked, in a didn't-work-at-all kind of way.

There were broom handle rod rests which snapped, or metal rod rests glued up with Araldite adhesive without the addition of Araldite hardener. One in particular stayed in my holdall for several seasons but never really set properly. Vince liked that one.

One item of shop-bought tackle that really offended me (but I must say probably worked as efficiently as if I'd made it myself) was my first swingtip. I remember someone telling Vince and I that the tackle shop in Ware was having a sale. Out of our skins with excitement, we hopped on a bus and went along with a few shillings in our pockets, intent on buying out the shop.

I have no idea what Vince came out with, but I was most taken with a swingtip that was reduced from 3/6d to just over a shilling. The front end was okay – a length of thin plastic with a couple of bent wire rings whipped to it. Then it kind of went off the rails a bit when it came to a short four-inch section of bendy see-through plastic which was jammed into the end. To complement the farce up that end, the final straw was a tiny piece of thick wire bent into a triangle shoved in the other end. This supposedly fitted over the rod tip. I can assure the person who designed it and the company who marketed it, that it didn't. Why the hell I persisted in using the thing for several seasons I wouldn't know. Whenever I hooked it over my rod tip and cast out it generally flew off the end and went sailing out into the lake with my end tackle.

I was in awe of the one Vince owned though – a supremely efficient one which actually screwed into the rod tip and didn't fly off at every cast. It did however have a ridiculous piece of semi-rigid pliable plastic that could be lengthened or shortened according to conditions and actually converted

when adjusted, into a quivertip. Trouble was, when it was adjusted to the short position, the long spare bit stuck out at an angle from the rod tip. Personally I thought it looked stupid so I just put up with mine which kept flying out into the lake – until I came up with the idea of Sellotaping it on. This however brought its own problems when the line kept snagging in the tip – although it did cure the problem of the swingtip heading out into the lake every cast. Only thing was, neither did anything else.

On one occasion, along the West Ham stretch of the River Lea, I got a real close-up view of Vince's swingtip when he smashed me across the face with it while striking a pound-and-a-quarter bream. In hindsight I suppose standing up in the reeds a rod length away from him, yawning at precisely the same moment he had his only bite of the day wasn't the most sensible thing I've ever done.

Then there was an interval of making my own sinkers. Small pieces of lead, from wherever I found them, were melted down in a tiny saucepan and then poured into the larger of two holes of, believe it or not, wooden clothes pegs. As I always used eighth-ounce leads, these were just the right size. Thinking back the only thing I can offer in my defence was that I was only twelve years old. Considering the amount of lead fumes I must have breathed in over Mum's cooker I'm surprised I made it to thirteen. I remember one particular day at school thinking I'd found Blackbeard's treasure when I walked out of the metalwork class with Vince with an

eight-and-a-half pound block of lead that I'd decided to take home with me hidden in my bag. Although I dragged it around school with me the whole day, it never got used.

Even well into my twenties, my inventiveness had not slowed down. Take my minnow trap scheme – although I'd had a brief flirtation with trying to make minnow traps out of bottles when I was about thirteen, all I succeeded in doing was smash the bottoms and half the sides out of all the wine bottles I'd been given.

But then, many years later, I needed some minnows. Thinking I could do something totally ingenious with a massive plastic plant propagator, I set about the thing with all manner of Stanley knives, hobby saws and cut-up plastic lemonade bottles. The finished article, well over two feet square, was tied together with string, glued with Araldite adhesive (this time with hardener added) and weighed down with several bricks, resembled some kind of futuristic Fritz Lang hamster theme-park.

I sneaked down to the little stream behind Barclay Park by the old ford at the dead of night and lowered the thing (with a load of bread inside) into the tiny pool just upstream of the footbridge. (When I was nine years old, my mate Peter Dyke informed me ghosts lived there and the pool was in fact bottomless. I used to look into the darkness and get giddy at the thought of the water just going on and on and on, trying to imagine what creatures might possibly be down there.) I'm afraid Pete really has a lot to

answer for – at best it was maybe two-and-a-half feet deep. No matter, I hid the strings and left the trap overnight to simply fill up with minnows.

I was due to meet Scotty at dawn so, well before light, I was down at the ghostly bottomless pool hauling out my multi-million minnow trap. All night I'd lain awake thinking I'd be awash with so many minnows I'd be releasing unwanted ones by the dozen.

Nothing was in it, not even the giant tentacled octopus that I believed lived down there when I was nine.

Return of the Swingtip

ABSURD IS PROBABLY the most appropriate word I can use regarding the first half-hour piking at Admiral's Walk that particular morning. I was twelve-years-old. Thankfully Pete, who was fishing with me that day, had wandered off somewhere so he was totally oblivious to the fiendish plan I was hatching as I reached into my little green bag …

For some reason, I'd latched on to something that Keith, another of my mates, had said previously – that swingtips were a deadly way of fishing for pike and that mackerel were quite simply *the* bait to use. He'd supposedly caught a twelve-pounder on one with his dad, so he obviously knew what he was talking about, and because a twelve-pounder was near enough as long as I was, it had set my mind off on all kinds of chaotic tangents.

So the next day I went along to Brewster's, the fishmongers at Hoddesdon (which used to be in one of the shops that our favourite tackle shop, Johnson Ross, expanded into) and there before me, laid out on the slab, was one of the largest mackerel I'd ever seen. It was also the only one, so I used up all my pocket money on the bloody thing. I actually remember weighing it on Mum's scales as I thought it might have been over the current British record, but no matter, looking over my shoulder for Pete I now lifted it out of my bag and unwrapped it. It looked even bigger than it did on the slab.

Hitching up the Mitchell 314 to the corks of my 5 ft spinning rod I threaded the line through the bent wire rings, down through the little swingtip from hell (yes the same one) and tied on the Jardine 'Snap Tackle' I'd bought specially. The swingtip fell off. Then it fell off some more so I gave up on it and busied myself with trying to attach the mackerel. The hook in the shoulders went in easily enough but I ended up having to hammer two prongs of the other treble into the back of its head with a rock. With the swingtip now balancing precariously on the rod tip, I hooked my finger over the line, opened the bail arm and went to lift the mackerel in preparation for its maiden flight.

I couldn't lift it.

Before I could even think of a plan B, I had to try and prise the hooks out of the back of its head. Setting about them with a knife, and now hardly resembling anything Mr Jardine ever had in mind, they came out. I sawed the head off, hammered the hooks back in again, and this time, together with the swingtip, the whole lot flew out into the lake. But after a couple more attempts and discovering patience I never knew I had, I finally managed to place the mackerel head where I wanted it. As an added bonus, the swingtip now quietly hung from the rod tip vaguely pointing in the right direction.

My thoughts drifted back to the previous weekend when, at the same spot, Dad and I had heard strange, muffled, subterranean squealing coming from under the path right next to us. Puzzled as we quietly listened and watched, we noticed the face of a stoat appear at the entrance of a rabbit burrow directly above the water. Startled by our presence he quickly dived back underground to resume his hunting beneath the path.

For this reason alone I'd wanted to return to the same spot, which is why I now sat there, idly looking at that stupid plastic swingtip which, inexplicably, was now dead straight and threatening to tow my rod into the lake with it. I grabbed the corks of my little rod, gripped the 314 and made to wind. Of course it didn't – the pike on the other end was seeing to that, and I could only imagine its surprised irritation as it wrestled with its prized meal, wondering why the hell it wouldn't move. And the reason it couldn't move was me at this end, mirroring its efforts with a tangled swingtip which defied all my attempts in freeing the line.

This ridiculous state of affairs continued until the pike, obviously blessed with less patience than I had, gave up any misplaced ideas of eating that morning and left me wondering why on earth anyone would believe swing-tipping was a good way to fish for pike. I'll never know how big the pike was – it could well have been nearly as long as me, but in reality it was probably only a murderous little two-pounder. The swingtip, the knots and the tangles stayed with me for several seasons, but that was the first and last time I ever used it for pike.

Horsehair and Bent Pins

I'M NOW SITTING beside yet another fishing friend, Colin Nobes. We're at Pretty Lake in Stanstead Abbotts in the most glorious tench swim you could imagine. A rainbow arches down on Colin's side of the lake. We're getting eaten alive by mosquitoes and the reason we're giggling like a couple of five-year-olds is because I'm leaning forwards in my chair, holding an 8 ft garden cane, and struggling to flick out a tiny porcupine quill further than the six feet of fine string will allow.

Little text messages keep trickling in from Scotty and Vince who are out in France fishing for monster carp with Steve Lotcho and his son Rob, and Vince's son, George. News comes through that Scotty's just caught yet another two obscenely large fish while Vince is sitting behind three cobwebbed rods.

To understand the reason why I'm now sitting here holding this ridiculous piece of cane we have to go back about fifty years – to a day when Mum took

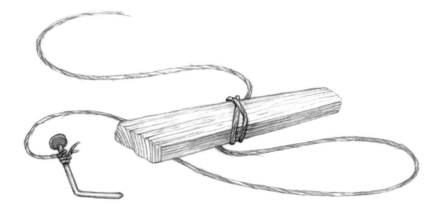

me for a walk around Barclay Park. I was seven and I stood there intrigued, watching a couple of kids, both younger than I, trying to fish. Their hand-lines consisted of lengths of furry parcel string, to which were looped 6-inch pieces of firewood. Two feet below these makeshift floats were tied 3-inch nails – the only difference in their set-ups was that one of the nails had been bent to a right angle while the other was dead straight. I remember vividly one of the kids trying to shove the straight nail through a poor, unfortunate, worm which fell in pieces to the ground.

Moving the story on twenty-five years to 1988 (a year or so after the Johnson's took over Ross's in Hoddesdon) Anthony, Matt and Lewis Johnson for some reason believed I was a master fisherman and could catch fish from a puddle. I don't know where this rumour came from or why they were so keen to spread it around. But over the last twenty-five years I've either lost this debatable reputation, or Anthony and his brothers got tired of repeating it.

But what stuck in my head and just couldn't be shaken loose however hard I tried, was the idea of catching a fish on horsehair and a bent pin. So this became the task I set myself. The bent pin was easy enough, and to give myself a chance, I decided on using some thin entomological pins. It was simple enough to bend a few of these into vague hook-like shapes with a pair of forceps. Next I needed some horsehair.

Again, thinking back many years I recalled that horses and I were never the best of company. (I was once stampeded over a cliff by a horse driven towards me by the same Pete who had seen me struck by the meteorite.) The idea of getting friendly with and distracting the front end of any kind of horse while I set about the tail with a pair of scissors was not something I relished, so I enlisted the help of yet another mate, Jason Inskip. Jason's daughter, Steph, kindly distracted her pony, Porridge, long enough to do the deed, and a few days later a nice twirl from Porridge's tail arrived in the post. Although my wife Pietra is a hairdresser, I wasn't about to ask her for lessons in French plaiting horsehair so I just did

whatever I thought looked right, and after a few hours ended up with half-a-dozen traces.

So here we are, Colin and I, sitting back watching the little porcupine quill underneath which is a horsehair trace and bent pin baited with a nice wriggly red maggot. Well, that's what I was doing – Colin was busy enough with his own tackle, untangling yet another knot he'd got himself into, muttering that now I knew why he stuck to carp fishing.

At first I thought nothing in its right mind would come close enough to the bank in front of us, but after five minutes of trickling maggots around the float, something decided to take a chance. The float sailed under and, amazingly, what appeared to be a small perch came flying out of the water and fell back in. Spurred by this almost instant success, my initial thoughts were of Vince over in France, four days into his trip without a fish on the bank. After missing two more bites, everything went right and I swung in a four-inch roach. Elated by my success at having caught a fish on horsehair and a bent pin, I went on to even greater things when, on my next cast, I caught a five-inch perch.

Colin dutifully took a few photos, and while Vince's son, George, was out in France doing battle with a seventy pound catfish, I was as happy as I've ever been – especially knowing that very soon my reputation around Hoddesdon, such as it is, would be restored.

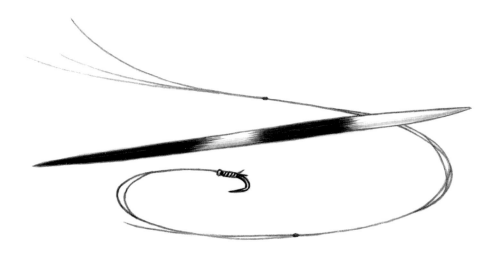

BAITING UP

I leave it to them to play at being sundials in their swims, watching their shadows lengthen and shorten.

Excuse Me, There's a Sprat in My Soup

A SILLY LITTLE episode but, when I look back, I remember it as clearly as if it were this morning. I hold it up as my offering to illustrate how profoundly silly I can be at times.

It must have been around 1968 when I was thirteen and my mind was awash with thoughts of pike. Sadly it wasn't awash with any amount of intelligence as I stood by the cooker that Saturday morning, stirring Mum's good saucepan containing what looked and smelled like a prop from a Hammer film. Every now and then it frothed up and steamed over the sides.

On the previous Friday afternoon a last-minute opportunity presented itself to go fishing. I'd run down to the fishmongers and caught old Albert just as he was hosing down the slab and closing up. The fresh sprats had gone and all he had left was a 2 lb bag of frozen ones. I'd never seen frozen sprats before and although I was unfamiliar with the rock hard bag he placed in my hands, at least it meant I could go fishing.

'Put them in the freezer section inside the fridge until you need to go, they'll be fine.' I ran back, did as I was told and started counting the minutes until I could go fishing. Life really didn't get better than this.

I don't know why I was so determined to catch the 3 a.m. bus to Turnford on this particular snowy Saturday, especially as it meant that I'd be standing in my pyjamas by the fridge at half-past-one in the morning holding this stupid icy, granite-like block of sprats.

I tried chiselling one side of it with the bread knife. One of the heads and a bit of tail fell on the floor with a tinkling clunk. Panic began overriding any reasoning I was born with and from among a bunch of useless alternatives, defrosting them presented the best option. I really don't know where this brainwave came from but I crammed the solid block of sprats in the saucepan, filled up what space was left with water and turned the gas on.

At first the block didn't stir, it just stayed wedged. After a very long while and many pokes with a wooden spoon the solid angular lump of grey ice actually began moving around the saucepan a bit, and I began to think I was getting somewhere.

The kitchen windows were beginning to steam up but at least it helped blot out the snow falling in the darkness outside. And as twenty-five pairs of sprat eyes watched me from within the melting lump of ice I couldn't help but wonder what the hell they were thinking as they gurgled from view beneath a frothy slurry of scales. Suddenly I realised I was probably only ten seconds from turning the whole lot to broth, so I poured it all out into the sink. Thankfully half of what was left bore some resemblance to

pike bait, albeit marginally, and my enthusiasm was raised long enough for me to quickly kick off my pyjamas, get dressed and head off to catch the 3 a.m. to Turnford. Oblivious to any of this farce, Mum and Dad slept on.

Snow had been falling heavily during the night and in the eerie silence mine were the only tracks through Hoddesdon as I arrived at the bus stop. I had no way of knowing that forty-four years later, my son Douglas would have been able to pull back the curtains and look at me waiting in the snow from his bedroom window – I was only a few yards away from Burford Place where he now lives. Burford Place is a row of delightfully old flint cottages built in 1872, only nine years before the gunfight at the OK Corral in Tombstone, Arizona.

As the single-decker bus appeared through the gloom, the illuminated snowflakes in the headlights seemed as large as half-crown pieces. I hopped on and as I chatted to the driver he continually questioned my sanity, and after the slow twenty-minute drive to Turnford, dropped me off. To this day, the mile-and-a-half of road between Wormley and Turnford High Road remains an enigma to me. Even now, no matter how many times I end up at any one point along it, something weird happens to my sense of direction, and whatever I do, I always end up heading the wrong way. Just like that morning when I stood there watching the bus drive off into a blizzard, realising too late that I'd got off a stop too early.

I knew I needed to find Slipe Lane, and although my brother Doug had taken me down there a couple of times I couldn't work out where it was. I headed off in completely the opposite direction. After a few hundred yards though nothing looked familiar, so I retraced my tracks and ended up back in the same spot. Of course there was no-one around to ask which way so I was just stuck there without a clue. I knew I needed to find the river so I aimed myself where I thought it was and made off towards it. I was beginning to think someone must have moved the bloody thing because all I could find was a housing estate with roads spidering off in every direction. I tried a few but ended up back to where I was originally. I tried further along the High Road and then cut back in again. This must have been Wharf Road and, after who knows how long, I'd crossed a railway line and was completely lost in a snowy, deserted wasteland. I wandered around for ages and, little did I know, if I'd continued a few yards at this point I would have found the river. However, given there was no way on earth anything I did that morning was going to be right, I turned round and dragged myself back to the High Road. I gave up, crossed the road and just walked anywhere until I found a bus stop. And there I stood, still in darkness, waiting for the next bus to take me home. I have no recollection as to what time I made it back but I seem to remember waking up to Mum opening my bedroom door …

'I thought you were getting up early to go fishing.'

A Few Pieces of Flake

IT'S MAYBE BECAUSE I spend most of my life painting subjects that can take anything up to a month and more to complete that I have little patience for anything else.

One exception perhaps is the little bit of patience I take with me along with my carp rod, but it's in precious short supply. Other than a loaf of bread, most of what I'm carrying with me as I approach the lake is a bucket load of impatience.

I've never lost touch with the little boy I always was and consequently I've never lost touch with the way I used to fish. No matter what I am fishing for I have never been more comfortable than when my bait is sitting close in front of me – at most, maybe a couple of rod lengths out, preferably under a float.

Like carp I share a fascination with lily pads and submerged trees and it's lucky for me that carp feel protected and safe in these secluded areas. It is precisely because of this that their guard will be down as they gather in the one or two areas of a lake where they won't be bothered by the likes of us.

And because I like to think I don't think quite like all the others wandering above the waterline, it allows the carp and I, quietly and intimately, to get to know each other a little better.

Watching carp in these situations it really didn't take long to realise it's not the bait they are wary of – it's the actual placement of it which alerts their suspicions. Quite simply, a bait a few inches outside their safety blanket is more often than not totally ignored. Drop it ever so slightly nearer and they might literally fight each other to get to it.

I don't need any more complicated tackle than the 11 ft split cane Chapman Mk IV which was lovingly made by my dear friend Dennis Gander, and a centrepin reel. The only thing I attach to my line, apart from a strong hook, is a tiny porcupine quill set at roughly the same depth as the swim – usually no more than five or six feet. For bait a little bit of flake will cover any eventuality that arises when I am within whispering distance of an unsuspecting carp. And as every situation is different and every swim unique it affects how I squeeze that piece of flake on my hook.

Around the lake at Nazeing there are many overhanging and submerged trees, not all of which will have carp in attendance. Some will at various times of course, but those I'm really interested in are the secluded areas which I call 'holding spots'. These can be found easily enough on clear water days when carp in numbers can be seen arriving and leaving and continually milling around. In these situations a piece of flake gently swaying and falling between the fish will, on most occasions, be taken without hesitation. Like a group of chub with one of my lobworms drifting down between them, one of the carp will have to make a grab before one of the others does. Should the flake actually make it to the bottom without being taken, a few loose pieces which I flick in will be enough to get them interested enough to follow them down to the gravel where they come to rest – with my bait amongst the loose pieces just waiting.

It is now that my eyes will keep flicking back to my little quill which is quietly lying flat on the surface above them. If the water is clear it is easy enough to actually watch the bait be taken, but if there are a lot of carp milling around, the flake will frequently be blotted from view. By constantly watching the float, it's a simple matter to know when the bait has been picked up as it zips forward an inch or dips under.

Over the last few years, Vince, Scotty, Steve and Colin have drifted towards the more relaxed approach to carp fishing, and as it's not really in my nature to spend hours and hours waiting for something to happen, I leave it to them to play at being sundials in their swims, watching their shadows lengthen and shorten.

All this was in the back of my mind one fateful morning as Vince and I approached the secluded corner amongst the trees. Fresh in my mind was an episode a few days previously when I surprised a monstrous mirror carp of 31 lb 6 oz that took a tiny piece of flake on the drop just the other side of the trees we were now looking at. As we stood there I asked Vince which side of the swim he wanted to sit. Given there was hardly enough room for a sunbathing squirrel, let alone both of us, he deliberated for a few seconds and, as there was an extra foot or so of space on the left, left it was. As he busied himself with taking the rucksack off his back and arranging a rod rest, I put my rod together, squeezed a piece of flake round the hook and flicked it over to the right on the outside edge of a load of branches. I suppose it took the bait ten seconds to feather down to the bottom, whereupon my little porcupine quill began to cock, lift half-an-inch, then fell back as it was. In the time this had happened Vince had blinked maybe three times as he rummaged inside his bag.

When he looked up, the unwelcome sight of my rod curled-over came as no real surprise, given that I've pulled this little trick on him no end of times over the years. He had just enough time to put the landing net together as I brought the fish towards it. Another immaculate mirror carp, this time weighing an incredible 35 lb.

The carp swam off happily after its release and Vince continued with his rummaging. I squeezed another piece of flake around my hook and flicked it out again. I think it had probably drifted down a couple of feet before the float zipped forward an inch. I struck, and as I turned to look at Vince, he was just threading his line through the second ring. Without wishing to labour the point the carp (this time a glorious common of 15 lb 4 oz with scales like big bronze coins) headed our way to be ultimately netted and released. Vince then finally finished his setting-up but at the precise moment of actually casting a bait in the water the weather suddenly turned for the worse and things closed down for the day.

I'm not so naive to think fishing in this way will always be so productive but when occasions arise and the conditions are just right, even a couple of hours creeping around the trees will see that little quill moving on almost every cast.

How I squeeze the flake around my hook depends on the swim I'm fishing, how many fish I'm expecting are present and, equally important, how I want it to behave as it enters the water. A large fluffy piece from a tin loaf will always float, and if I quickly dip it in the water before I flick it out, I can easily cast it thirty yards if needs be. Should I see, for example, a sneaky carp approach from the other side of the bay along the top, then this is what I'll do. If it's not taken on the surface quite often he will follow it down as it starts to sink. If he doesn't take it though it will frequently be taken by a second carp following a couple of feet further down. A tiny piece flattened around the heavy hook will sink gently, wavering as it feathers down to the bottom. Several loose fluffy pieces floating around under overhanging branches can make a shoal of wary sunbathing carp go bananas. Even if these fish weren't thinking about feeding, preferring rather to rest up for the afternoon, half-a-dozen pieces of floating flake are often too good to pass up. And if they don't fancy them floating on the top, then the same amount wafting around on the bottom will have them doing exactly the same thing down below.

I fished the same secluded woody swim on another occasion, though this time my companion was Scotty. Anglers were dotted around the

lake, laid out on bed-chairs like seals taking in the sun, sleeping mostly, their lifeless lines cheese-cutting into open water, arrowed down to baits attached to heavy leads amongst mountains of hundreds upon hundreds of identical baits. Nothing much was happening, even in our swim, where we were both float fishing up against the trees.

As usual, the niggles began setting in, so I got up and ambled off to the left of Scotty. Between us and the next swim, called 'Brollies', and which itself was very tight and secluded, was a great canopy created by ancient overhanging willows that had half toppled in over the years. Still growing out from the bank, these half-submerged trunks, branches and leaves criss-crossed in and out of the water like a tangle of Everglades mangroves. As

I passed along the old gravel bank several feet higher up, I glanced down amongst the branches into a narrow clear section of water, probably no bigger than 15 ft by 8 ft. In shards of sunlight I could see the water was only a couple of feet deep. Then, as if conjured up in my own mind, a carp quietly drifted through. Then another … and another. I went back to my swim and gathered my rod, landing net and a loaf of bread.

I was back in less than a minute and not wishing to sit right on top of the fish as they cruised through the gap not ten feet from the water's edge I hid myself amongst a tangle of ivy twelve feet up the sloping bank. The mass of ivy growing over a fallen log made a nice backrest as I settled into it.

I set my porcupine quill at only two foot deep and, placing a small piece of flake around my hook, took care to make sure it was going to sink immediately. Because of the height above the water, the awkwardness of the enclosed space I was in and the twigs and leaves which seemed to grab at me whenever I pulled a coil of line off my centrepin, my first three casts went everywhere except where I intended. Fortunately the carp took no notice, and still they cruised through in twos and threes. I was in the mother of all holding spots and no amount of stuffing things up could distract them from feeling completely at home and safe from all the snoozers around the lake.

Finally getting everything right, the flake landed perfectly with my quill following its descent, then laying flat and motionless on the surface. Clouds passing the sun darkened the water in front of me, causing the highlighted forms of drifting carp to ghost from view. Even without the sun filtering through the canopy I could still make out my piece of white flake nestling among dark leaves on the gravel. With the close proximity of the bait and my quill just above it I could easily watch both at the same time.

The flake blotted out, the quill moved an inch. My strike met with thin air and all I was rewarded with was a tangle of everything beyond my rod tip snarled up through the ivy leaves. My next five or six casts and strikes were a repeat of the first thin-air one, and it was painfully apparent that my angle of strike from such an awkward position was anything but right. Extricating myself from the wretched wall of ivy, I decided to join the carp. I slid forward to a point where I was almost sitting on top of them. Dropping my next piece of flake below the rod tip, I sat in wait for the next arrival. Within seconds the very next carp, casually cruising through, picked up the bait. A little snick of the rod tip and the boiling churn of water left me in no doubt whatsoever that I would simply have to hold on. In these situations if you quickly counter every twist and turn with a pull from another angle to disorient the fish, they can be drawn over the net almost before they know what has happened.

Hearing the commotion from next door, Scotty ran round, skidded down the bank and netted the fish just as it was beginning to think about ruining my day by joining the mallards out in the open water beyond the trees. A truly wonderful common carp of 19 lb, we watched as it swam off looking slightly puzzled.

Convinced I'd just sent every carp within a hundred yards not only to the other side of the lake, but also across the path and into the adjacent lake, I nevertheless tied up a new hook and flicked out a few pieces of flake into the earthquake zone which once was my swim. Truth be told, experience has taught me not to be surprised at anything that happens in these holding spots. Two huge mirrors immediately drifted through from my left and began picking at the pieces of flake. As I squeezed a new piece around my hook ready to flick it out, they glided through the shadows to my right. Seconds too late the bait hit the water and wavered down to the gravel behind them. Within a few seconds though, new beams of sunlight illuminated the golden mailed flank of a carp which I hadn't known was there, following the mirrors. As he inched forward, the light in front of me illuminated the form of an immense common carp which unconcernedly drifted over to the white halo of flake that was lying in front of him. With as much confidence as if he had moved over to a few caddis fly larvae, he sucked in the bait and continued on his way.

The quill cocked slightly but before it could turn and dip under to follow the fish, I swept the rod over to my left. There was no reaction whatsoever as the carp simply carried on his leisurely amble through to my right. Easily weighing forty pounds, I gasped as he continued towards a large willow trunk arching out from the bank and into the water under the canopy. With my rod curling round into a bow, and just as he was about to pass under the trunk, the carp swung round to face me. Showing as much irritation as a cow would shrug off a fly, he shook his head and my line fell slack. Looking into his eyes I imagined I could see puzzlement in his face, as he fanned his fins, slowly turned on the spot and faded from view under the trees, no doubt wondering what had happened.

Cheese Puffs

ONE LITTLE EPISODE concerning a particular carp in Nazeing requires me to run a lot of line off the reel as I travel back quite a few years. I suppose Chad and I were both in our early twenties. Those of you reading this who have reached the point of obsession that we had at this stage will understand completely. For several years Chad, Vince and I were catching incredible numbers of carp on nothing more elaborate, secretive, or sinister, than Sainsbury's cheese puffs. We roped my good friend Bob Jermy into all of this and between the four of us we must have caught nearly every carp in the lake – or so it seemed. Except one in particular which, at the time, happened to be one of the largest – a large leather carp of around 19 lbs. I'd had no trouble hooking it – I could've done that in my sleep – however Fate, for whatever reason, didn't want me to land it.

Armed with dozens of bags of cheese puffs we used to descend on the lake and after drifting armadas of these things across the surface the place at times looked like a stew pond of starving trout such were the numbers of feeding carp. Under the trees it took nothing more than threading a cheese puff on the hook and flicking it out and you were in. If the fish were further

out, a running half-ounce Arlesey bomb on the line, stopped a few inches from the hook by a leger-stop, did the trick. A longish cast amongst rising fish, the rod tip was quickly sunk an inch or two and the slack taken up, then the bail arm was opened and the buoyant yellow cheese puff would rise up to the surface. Immediately to be inspected by the nearest carp … and moorhen, mallard, coot and seagull.

Dad would join me at times and sit beside me with a pair of binoculars telling me when to strike. On seeing a large swirl at the bait, it was easy to strike into thin air as the yellow cheese puff would often be masked by a carp rolling over it. On these occasions we realised that the bait hadn't been actually taken, but at a distance it was difficult to judge. After many missed takes we discovered the defining moment would simply be a quick glance beyond the rod tip. The bow in the line lifting slightly would be the time to strike.

114

The big leather carp I was after could always be counted on to appear in front of us, especially when we fished the 'Platform'. After a while, watching his friends boiling and swirling at loose cheese puffs out in the open water, the carp would come out from under one of the two submerged willows which flanked the swim on either side. He would often get so preoccupied with the cheese puffs that he would swim around with half his back showing and he'd slurp down everything in front of him with a noise you could hear half-way around the lake. Whenever he lined up the cheese puff he wanted – often from yards away – he'd cruise over to it with a bow wave like a killer whale and finish the thing off in a boiling swirl. The bow of the line lifting was the moment to strike and one day, after I'd missed numerous attempts, I finally found myself securely attached to the carp of my dreams.

With only a very light carp rod and 7.3 lb Platil 'Strong' line, I didn't have too much say in things as, like a kite on a string, the carp continued on his way quite unconcerned into the dead willow branches about forty feet out in the lake to my left and knitted himself in.

Nothing I could do would tempt him out. Every time I gave him line he took yards and yards and then, on retrieving it all, instead him heading out into open water, he'd return to the same spot in the tree, looped round a branch with no way of getting him loose. Unless of course I went in myself.

So I did. I handed Chad the rod, stripped down to my pants and taking my landing net out with me swam over to the tree following the line which was pulling through my hand. Eventually I ended up treading water with the line going directly down between my legs. I kept pulling and pulling but time and time again the line just snaked off around the unseen branch way below me. No matter what I did the result was the same. Eventually, and given it was all I could do to keep my head above water by this time, I gave the line a final jerk. And like magic the cat's cradle unwound and the line and hook came free … sadly minus the carp. I managed to swim back dragging my landing net swirling behind me, just in time to stick a couple of fingers up at Chad who was taking photos of the whole sorry event.

A few days later the whole stupid episode was re-enacted when the carp came along once again, took my bait, and like a homing pigeon going to roost, swam straight back into the same tree. Mistakenly thinking things would end differently this time I went in again. They didn't. One good thing I suppose, I was no wetter the second time than the first.

Shortly after I'd resigned myself to never seeing this fish on the bank, Steve finally cured my obsession when he caught it one night. It weighed 18 lb 4 oz.

If Steve saved me any more impromptu swimming with the capture of that carp, he most certainly got things stirred again with his mention of another one. Nazeing in the early days was home to many small wild carp. Looking almost like barbel, the 'wildies' weighed around the four pound mark and although we caught countless numbers of them, I don't think I ever saw one in my net that went to five.

And so it was when Steve called me round to the 'Gate Swim' one dark autumn evening – I was in awe as I photographed him with one of 6 lb 3 oz. A truly wonderful fish which in the torchlight held me spellbound. When he mentioned that there was reputed to be one swimming around in the region of 18 lb, I didn't believe him. I'd never seen anything remotely close to that size in all the outings and all the seasons I'd fished there. Nevertheless we all lived in hope of meeting up with this carp however implausible it may have seemed.

Then one day we were back at the deep bank at Nazeing. It was a lovely hot sunny day and I was just putting my tackle down behind Vince who was looking out across the lake.

'Let's fish here. I reckon this'll be okay.'

Although we were standing under a gigantic ancient willow tree which grew out from the bank to our left, the whole area of water in front of us, the whole lake in fact, was as clear as anything and in the region of twenty feet deep.

As we prepared our tackle I drifted out some cheese puffs and within

minutes a few carp had found them and were swirling thirty yards out. Because of the depth of water in this area of the lake, we'd intended to fish on the bottom, but the pull of watching carp take cheese puffs was too much for me – off came the bottom tackle and on went the running Arlesey bomb. A long cast and the wait for the lead to hit bottom, followed by another achingly-long wait for the cheese puff to come up. Several casts to get everything to behave properly, and finally my bait was out in the middle of nowhere, just breaking surface and waiting. Within seconds there was a massive swirl and I could feel the weight of a heavy carp as it powered off down to the bottom. Because of the tight area on the bank Vince wound his rod in to give me a little more space and readied himself with the net as I continued to play the fish. For ages it stayed out in open water. My Mitchell was just a dream and my Platil Strong was holding well and eventually the carp began to rise up in the water. About two feet below the surface it turned in the sunlight. A huge, impossibly long, golden flank rolled, turned down and began heading our way – a wildie, maybe even the eighteen-pounder. Then down, down into the roots of the willow it plunged. As the line cut through the water my rod tip clawed round following it as it powered ever onward to somewhere I really didn't want it to go.

There was nothing I could do but watch my line where it entered the water, juddering and grinding to a halt somewhere down to our left. And there it stopped. Cursing at how I couldn't keep it near the surface when it first rolled, I knew that how ever much I wanted to play things out in the open water, a wildie this size could do pretty much whatever it wanted to.

For a good five minutes I tried everything I knew to get it moving, but to be honest I was half convinced it was gone, lost amongst the roots. On about my millionth pull, something gave way and inexplicably the line came to life once more and began cutting out into the lake. Incredulous, we both watched as, once again, the fish returned to clear water, where I was adamant it was going to stay until it reached the net. Then for no reason any angler would ever understand, it decided it preferred to be back in the tree and turned round, took a deep breath and swam straight back into the willow roots.

I was resigned once again to watching my line pluck, grind and twist in ever decreasing circles as the magnificent fish sewed the roots together again.

My one remaining nerve was on a knife-edge waiting for that awful moment when the rod springs back, when the unthinkable happened again. I'm absolutely sure that carp was the more surprised of the two of us when, as he headed back out into the open, he found he was still attached. Everything was free, the line, the fish and, with all the branches, roots and snags behind him, he headed back out towards the main lake. And it is here where I may as well end this little story because it is precisely at this point that Vince discovered powers he never knew he had.

As my rod was bending over, and the sunlight was cascading through the surface ripples, and as the tautness in my line, holding alive a million dreams of a million anglers, headed out into the far, far beyond … Vince spoke:

'I reckon if you were going to lose that you'd have lost it by now.'

The precise moment my hook came flying back at me was when Vince uttered the word 'lost'.

None of us ever saw that fish again and for all we know he may well still be out there. In all these intervening years the carp at Nazeing have grown and grown, with some of their number reaching over an incredible forty pounds.

Whether or not that carp was a true wildie we'll never know. Maybe, or even more likely, it was an extraordinarily long king carp, maybe weighing eighteen pounds, maybe over twenty, but none of it really matters. What does are the memories it gave me. The passing of time, days on end of dreaming and wondering, re-living moments and imagining what might be every time the line tightens.

And if and when it does, I'm left wondering whether Vince is picking his moment to utter those words again …

The Man With No Bait

DAVE EVANS. I'M sure the very name strikes fear in the hearts of all bait manufacturers. Dave, who is on first name terms with every maggot in his bait box, can turn the last sandwich in his bag into the entire bait supply on his next trip.

You have to understand this to fully appreciate the ambling figure as he approaches – carrying little more than a rod, chair and a Sainsbury's bag with a rod rest sticking out of it. The rod being the only clue that he is actually going fishing, as opposed to someone just taking a plastic bag for a walk. Which in fact he may as well be, because although he goes through the motions with the passion, intent and conviction of a Swiss watchmaker (which is not surprising as he is one of the country's finest antique restorers), fish, it seems, will go through most of their lives without ever making his acquaintance.

So here I am with Dave at Rye Meads. It's a lovely evening and we're sitting side-by-side amongst some nice reeds, our rod tips angled closely by the water's surface. Our peacock quills are just two feet further out, waiting for the perfect tench to arrive, preferably hungry. I turn to my good friend:

'Dave, you got any maggots on you?'

'Yes, mate.'

With that he leans down, rustles around in his half-empty Sainsbury's bag which is shoved into a heap of wild mint and mud and, while I'm pouring out coffee, he pulls out the tiniest plastic bait box the world has ever seen. The top is two-and-a-half inches across.

I suppose my expression must have been equal to his as we both looked inside. There were two brittle, dried-up black casters stuck to the plastic by a crumb of groundbait, while a single lonely maggot was doing its best to evade his prying fingers by hiding under the two black shells. As I handed Dave a coffee, some of it spilt straight over the maggot, killing it instantly.

I can honestly say I felt sorry for the poor thing, and actually tried to manipulate some life back into it. Here my memory fades a little as I can't remember if I managed it or not. If I did, given the way I am, I would have let it go. If it remained dead, I'm sure one of us would have used it, but as we caught nothing in any case, none of it would have mattered.

Unbelievably or, rather, believably, Dave has accumulated three hundred hours of fishing time at Rye Meads without success. Success in the way of bites or fish that is, but as always with us, success isn't just measured by fish in the net – which in Dave's case is just as well.

Then, wonder of wonders, I saw Dave at Rye Meads one evening and he was kneeling over a landing net. I have to admit I was seriously taken aback by what I saw. The figure was familiar enough but the fact that he was peering into a landing net and unhooking a tench of over 7 lb shook me somewhat. I hate to admit it, but I may have looked around for anyone else who may have actually caught it. The tench had taken a large cube of buoyant breadcrust fished lift-style right under his rod tip. No doubt from a piece of his sandwich. Buoyed by the reality of actually catching a fish for once, he went on to even greater things and, incredibly, caught another two large tench a few days later. I think that Dave got a little above himself though and things soon returned to normal. Cuckoos returned in the Spring, closely followed by martins and swallows. Warblers arrived to sing amongst the blossoms and Dave went back to watching his float.

This state of fishlessness was, to my recollection, only ever broken once more. Scotty and I were tackling up in 'Shrews' on the Big Turnford pit when Dave's eternally surprised voice came floating through from next door:

'Blimey, I'm in.'

So rarely used to hearing this, I walked round to find him standing at the water's edge in the darkness with his rod curled over, playing a fish. For once, the Man With No Bait had really lived up to his name. Plumbing the depth of water close in, in front of him, with nothing on his line other than a peacock quill, shot and a hook, he'd dropped the whole rig straight into the mouth of a pike which was now flying round all over the place. Eventually landed, it weighed at a bit over nine pounds. I'm still at a loss today about who was most surprised – Dave, Scotty, myself or the pike.

After returning the fish he'd forgotten about plumbing his swim, and fully two hours after it was light, he stood up, looked where his bait was and found he'd been fishing in two feet of water.

Great-Uncle Fidenzio's Secret Weapon

AND NOW, LET'S wander back to Great-uncle Fidenzio's kitchen those many years ago and find out what was in the secret box.

I won't admit to being quite knocked off my chair by the smell as he opened it but it was touch and go. As he opened the box, around twenty or thirty dry, brown, shrivelled insect bodies spilled out onto the table. As did this indescribable, incredible smell. At the time I thought they were dried cicadas, but several years later, after I got a slightly higher grade detective badge, I found out they were more properly, *crisalide del baco da seta*, or dried chrysalis of the silk moth.

They are sold in tightly sealed packages in Italian fishing shops as bait, specifically for carp, bream, chub and tench. About an inch long, in their dried form they will float, but when boiled as per the instructions on the packet, they will soften up and be useable as a bottom bait – if you can stand the smell.

Alternatively, if you have a kitchen about a mile-and-a-half from your main house, you can liquidise them, turn into a powder and use them to make a paste. To the adventurous among you in search of the Holy Grail of fishing baits, I will say look no more. There are ways of acquiring them from abroad and I will leave you to your own devices to obtain them.

I well remember the day I placed an unopened, sealed packet in Mum and Dad's luggage on our return trip to England. Even the addition of several layers of cling-film, aluminium foil and plastic bags didn't stop our clothes smelling like Great-uncle Fidenzio's kitchen for months.

Not the best idea I ever had.

FISHING

There can be little to beat sitting in the darkness on a warm drizzly autumn evening with an old cane rod resting across my knee and my finger crooked over the line by the centrepin.

Ernie the Acting Eel

AS I WALKED along the towpath I realised how little things had changed in these forty years, although this time I was moving a little more slowly. In 1970, after school, Vince, Chad and I would cycle along this gravel path at breakneck speed to fish there. Even then the little pool next to the River Stort about half a mile above Feildes Weir was in a state of disrepair. Circular in shape and thirty feet across at most, it was more of an overspill from the Stort rather than a weir pool. Water spilled down over an ancient brick wall onto a narrow ledge before trickling into the pool.

One afternoon as we were cycling along the towpath, Vince and I happened on an eel of about a pound lying immobile at the edge of the river. I stopped to pick it up and carried it to the pool where I dropped it into the water. Totally immobile, dead still, as it were, but with nothing at all visibly wrong with it, Vince said it was just acting so, giggling like a couple of five-year-olds, we named it Ernie the Acting Eel. This was probably a follow-up to a pike we found at Nazeing about the same time which was obviously dead, but that Vince insisted was also only acting. This particular fishy thespian we named Oscar the Acting Pike.

The pool, which was quite a bit lower than the main river, was surrounded on all sides by old willows and hawthorns and didn't have much clear water to fish. This of course just added to the mystique of the place. My favourite was the ledge where I sat with my back against the old damp wall as the water from the Stort spilled around me. The outflow from the pool was nothing more than a ditch hidden from view by an impenetrable tangle of old dead bushes and trees.

Chad and Vince also had their favourite swims and it was great fun to fish for whatever might turn up as we talked to each other around the pool. Mostly we caught small roach and chub, together with the odd gudgeon, but one afternoon I hooked the most glorious, metallic-blue-scaled roach I've ever seen and weighing exactly one pound – bigger by far than any roach I'd previously caught. I missed my next bite but not the next – a chub of around the same weight as the roach flashed under the surface as it rolled off the hook. As Chad fished with lobworms, a few small pike of a pound or so kept him entertained on most trips.

One afternoon when I really should have been at school or, rather, at home being ill as I was supposed to be, the pull of the little weir got the better of me. I had four bites on my little porcupine quill that miserable wet afternoon, but the four roach I caught were between eight and twelve ounces each – as memorable an afternoon as I could ever have wished for.

So here I was again, the Stort looking the same even after all these years. The odd few houseboats were moored along the near edge, and the tangle of blackthorn bushes overhanging the opposite bank looked as tempting as ever. However, the promise of seeing the little pool again had me hurrying along the path. I arrived at a lock gate, surprised that I'd completely forgotten its existence. Never mind, I could see the outside of the bend about a hundred yards further up where I knew the pool to be.

As I approached and stood with the overspill under my feet, the old wall and the ledge looked exactly as I remembered. The trees were all the same but the passing of years had seen their branches grow and encroach all around the pool as if to protect the magic there. One of the old willows, growing so large, had finally given in to the inevitable and fallen into the centre of the pool. This effectively reduced what little fishing area there was to the immediate six feet or so where the water trickled in. Fortunately the willow had fallen in such a way as to form a tiny theatrical stage of water

enclosed within a crescent of branches just downstream where, if I wanted to trot a bait, I could drift it right down into the middle of the tree.

All I had with me though, was my wand-like 8ft Ribtickler (a mere whisp of carbon) and my trusty 308. I'd left my lobworms and floats at home, so opening the creel, I took out the smallest Mepps spinner I had. (Which, to be honest, was the same size as all the others I'd ever bought.)

I flicked it right into the crescent of branches, let it sink two inches and began to wind it back in. A solid thump and I was now attached to something which desperately wanted to get back into the tree. To my surprise it almost did, but as I curled my little rod over, the fish rolled on the surface – an immaculate chub of about two pounds. And, incredibly, mirroring its every twist and turn, were five others of equal size. As I readied it for the net, I delayed a few seconds and watched, mesmerised, as these other fish continued in their manic dance around their hooked brother.

I released it in the water, thinking I'd soon be catching all the others, but after twenty minutes I'd only managed to lightly hook one more which immediately fell off. Given the extreme restrictions of the swim it was obvious I was now wasting my time, so I left them to continue doing what they preferred to do in their tree.

My inevitable return a few days later saw me sneaking down beside the wall with a can of lobworms. Same rod but now matched with Dennis Gander's delectable centrepin, the Branta. I hooked-up one of my huge lobworms and set an orange-tipped Paul Cook perch float at about two feet deep. Within a few trots into the crescent, I'd made friends with several nice perch of around six ounces. With each bite and each perch, I became more and more puzzled as to where the chub had gone.

I inched Cookie's float towards the end of the crescent where it came to rest against some submerged twigs. I knew it was hung-up as it began to drag in the curl of the current. I left it for a few seconds, thinking a stationary bait might not be quite so attractive to the perch which had been picking it off as it moved through. I don't think I actually saw the float disappear but something surely happened as my little rod was now in the most impossible curve it had ever been in. The more I lifted, the more the rod hooped over, as whatever was down below most certainly wasn't in any mind to come up. As the line strained through the current, great clouds of silt came swirling up to the surface. In those electrifying first few moments I was Dick Walker and Clarissa, Chris Yates and The Bishop, The Old Man and The Sea. My tackle was sound but I had the impression all I was succeeding in doing was upsetting whatever I'd hooked. It was only at the point when the line began to cut towards me through billowing clouds of silt, that I dared allow myself the possibility that I might actually land the thing. Thinking I now had the upper hand, I wound right down and began to lift. I will admit to feeling very apprehensive at this point – not because I thought I might lose it, but at the thought of seeing what on earth I could have hooked.

One last lift and up and up and up it came, a huge grey eel – easily four pounds, probably more. For a full thirty seconds I somehow managed to keep its head and a foot of its length out of the churning water just below the sill. I had to grab the little cane landing net, realising now how pitifully small and inadequate it was – but even if it were larger, it wouldn't have made an iota of difference. In the stumbling few seconds while I tried to net it, the eel had gained some fresh momentum and had corkscrewed itself down to the bottom again. The writhing twisting shape retreated into the greyness amongst a swirling mass of bubbles and disturbed twigs, where my last glimpse was of its face and eye, before the pool reclaimed its king. A few seconds later the line finally parted and I reeled in. Perhaps I'm asking a little too much of my imagination, but maybe, just maybe, it was Ernie.

Tench on the Wrong Bait

THE PEACOCK QUILL settled on the surface, and laying flat, stayed there. Steve gave it a little flick with his line followed by another, neither of which did anything. Before he could get too puzzled it shot off and as his rod crawled over he realised his best ever tench of twelve ounces was about to become a distant memory.

The first reedy bay of the North Met was a favourite of ours and although it never really gave up any of its treasures to me, the black and white photograph of Steve with his tench of 3 lb 11 oz has remained one of the most memorable I've ever taken. Dad made an enlargement of it in his darkroom and for years I lived in awe of that fish. Although countless numbers of tench have since hit the net, many far, far, bigger, none of them have evoked feelings to stir me as that particular fish did.

Throughout the 1970s, our tench fishing took us to many different waters around Hoddesdon, Broxbourne and Cheshunt. And although ten years later we had a brief interlude of casting swimfeeders out to the edge of a weed bed in the big pit at Turnford, we were never happier than when we could idly sit back and watch a float close-in. Dave did this anyway just because he liked watching a float, even if there weren't any tench to be caught within thirty yards of it.

There's something just right about watching a float, and never is it more true than when fishing for tench. The quiet anticipation that builds up while watching a float lazily half-cocked against lilies in a forgotten reedy bay far outweighs any mild disappointment felt at the end of the day if the tench haven't shown. Quite simply, watching a float having life breathed in it by an inquisitive tench is, without doubt, one of the greatest pleasures in fishing. And if that float is a handmade Paul Cook, lovingly crafted from natural materials, then every bite is just that bit more memorable.

On 15 June, 2000, Scotty and I were at Toyhall Lake in Cheshunt. Relieved at finding our favourite swim on the end of the long spit unoccupied, we unhitched all our tackle in delicious anticipation of the perfect evening's fishing. We took it in turns raking out a clear area close in. The lilies weren't up yet, but huge banks of Canadian pond weed surrounded us on all sides and out in front of us.

As befitting a wonderful summer evening and such a perfect setting, the final touch, the only one we could possibly add, were our floats. These were fished three feet apart, lift-method style, about five feet deep just off our rod tips. Baits were small bunches of maggots. If our set-ups were identical then so too were our rods and reels – both 13 ft Normark 'Avengers' matched with a pair of lovely Richard Carter Aerials. In fact the only item of tackle to differ was the line. I was using my normal 5 lb Maxima while Scotty chose some other make, a little lighter in colour.

Everything was set, all we needed now was something to break the spell, and preferably not Scotty's torch blowing up in his face again.

A tench rolled close in and then a little later needle bubbles began showing on the surface in between the floats. I had no doubt in my mind that any moment I'd have a tench, a big tench, definitely, positively taking my bait.

It was 9.10 p.m. when Scotty's float started tilting and wavering gently. Within a few seconds it became obvious the fish below was showing serious intent on his bait, and not just feeding on loose offerings nearby and brushing the line in passing. Then Scotty's rod arched over.

To give him some room, I quickly reeled in my tackle, gathered my line and propped my rod out of the way over a small willow bush overhanging the water to my left. At this point let me admit to a rather lax and casual understanding of the words 'out of the way'. But back to Scotty, and with the fish beginning to get fed up with his efforts of trying to stop it burying itself into the edge of the weed bed, it turned and headed off on a run further out into the lake and buried itself into another weed bed instead. Much to Scotty's annoyance this is where it stayed and it was at this point he was pretty much resigned to losing it, especially as it seemed he was now attached to the never-ending bank of weed that covered most of the rest of the lake.

After quite some time of pulling and straining with the line though, the fish miraculously kicked itself free of the weeds and, still hooked, headed off to the left across my side of the spit and then disappeared through a mass of reeds and overhanging branches.

I was sandwiched between the willow bush on my immediate left and Scotty who was standing by my right boot with his rod clawing around my chest, and no room to move, even if I'd wanted to.

I was also juggling a landing net and attempting to stop his jarring rod from snagging amongst all the willow branches. I managed this to some extent but Scotty's fish decided at this stage to get busy itself … knitting and weaving and generally gathering up the line from my rod which I'd propped up in the bush. Things weren't going too well and noticing a large snarl of my line heading up towards his rod tip, I meekly said that I didn't hold out too much hope of a happy ending.

'Don't worry mate, I don't really think it's that big in any case.'

Scotty's words didn't really make me feel any better as we both knew at any second his line was going to give.

Unbelievably he managed to drag his rod tip clear of the bush and as we looked up at it in the failing light of a glorious sunset, a wren's nest of my line was now jammed in the end ring.

As nothing was going to be achieved by leaving it there, Scotty lowered his rod and I hesitatingly began to pick away at it. Given the farce since he hit the bite neither of us really expected me to achieve anything worthwhile but as we'd got this far with the fish still attached, I decided to bite away at the now completely matted knot of line. Luckily the difference in the colour of the two lines was such that all I needed to do was bite away at the darker line – my Maxima. A couple of minutes later everything came free and Scotty curled his rod back over and slowly drew the fish towards my waiting net.

M.J.PLEDGER.

I'd had a few glimpses of the tench (for this is what it was) during the drama, however Scotty still hadn't seen it with me standing in the way. It came as no small relief to either of us that it was now safely cradled in the mesh and as we gently unhooked it and placed it in the weigh sling, he still had no idea how big it really was. I had my own ideas and wanted to read out the weight without him seeing the dial. It was only when I swivelled it round and he saw for himself that it finally dawned on him – one of those moments for the sixpence jar. At ten pounds exactly it was quite simply the largest tench we'd ever seen and made even more special that we were together to share it.

And I still think it took the wrong bait.

The Bite

FOR ME, THE moment of magic.

The seed was without doubt sown all those years ago at the Giardini Margherita in Bologna when Mum held me over the higgledy-piggledy wall and I looked down at the boys' red plastic bobbers. Mum had no way of knowing, but it wasn't only the goldfish who were hooked. The very moment one of those little floats began to twitch and those tiny ripples circled out they captivated my mind completely and now, just as then, they continue to feed my imagination as I impatiently await the next fishing trip.

In this respect I'm sure I'm no different from any of you. For no matter how much we all dream, how many windows we may gaze through idly wishing away the hours until we're fishing again, the moment all our conquests begin, imaginary or otherwise, start with the magical moment of the bite.

I well remember one bitterly cold Boxing Day many years ago when I was determined to get out fishing. As I sat alone, shivering, at the overgrown little pond in Green Lane, Nazeing, I willed four almost-indiscernible ripples from my tiny porcupine quill. One I missed but the other three

yielded three identical tench of about a pound each. I'm sure that in the great scheme of things the event warrants nothing more than a cursory sniff, but those three tiny ripples mean more to me than the countless thousands of other bites that I've obviously forgotten about over the years.

The moments we all dream about can be as varied as pebbles on a beach. The dream depends on the fish we are after and the method we choose. The take from a nymphing trout in a rippling stream is far removed from that of a starving chub which has just cannoned into a big black slug that has landed behind his tail. A six-inch dace on a winter's morning could easily clean out a caster shell on a size 22 hook without you even knowing until you reel in. The same fish, and I can well vouch for it, has on occasion easily taken one of my ten-inch lobworms in one gluttonous thump and had I missed the bite, I would have been excused for thinking an eight pound barbel had been the culprit.

Using my sense of touch to feel a fish taking my bait is second only to watching the trembling of a bite on a porcupine quill. And the heart quickens as you intently watch the bow in your line as a fish runs and you carefully judge the moment to strike.

There can be little to beat sitting in the darkness on a warm, drizzly, autumn evening with an old cane rod resting across my knee, and my finger crooked over the line by the centrepin. Out in front of me, nodding in the gloom, is the little betalight on the rod tip. My head sometimes also nodding and on occasion jerking back slightly as I realise that yet again I've given in to sleep. A familiar and welcome tightening of the line over my finger tells me that interest is being shown in my free-lined bait. A series of trembles and plucks suggests that only a few feet away, under the canopy of floating watercress, a barbel is wandering through. In the same instant, my betalight becomes a shooting star heading under the canopy, accompanied by a solid thump of the line through my finger.

The moment of the bite, whether I'm now on the bank playing my fish, or lying in bed drifting into sleep, reliving it over and over again, is the moment in time that pervades my thoughts and keeps this gentle obsession with fishing alive.

My good friends Vince, Scotty, Steve and Colin have all given in to their own obsession of a running carp. If I look into their dreams I can understand their own anticipation in patiently waiting for the line to blur off the reel. I can appreciate the excitement when, maybe after several hours, the line, previously dead at the reel, bursts into life and cuts out into the lake. Their own hectic lifestyles allow them at last a few precious hours to sit back, relax and wait for it all to happen. Part of their dream is the intense build up and preparation for the trip and when they've arrived at their destination, the dream is allowed to continue at a leisurely pace while they take in the surroundings, watch the birds and just wait.

As for me – my dreams are festooned with porcupine quills. Maybe because I've caught so many trams and buses in Bologna, walked so many back doubles with Dad and entered time and time again, the same dusty old shops in search of the ultimate quill. With too many memories of lost sleep in anticipation of yet another morning being jostled and bounced around on the old grey bus and being dropped off on the cobbled streets in the searing heat, for the reward of seeing a simple plain glass tumbler on the counter containing maybe just a couple of them.

Call it an obsession or perhaps a recurring desire to relive the formative days of my life, to watch a simple tiny quill as it lies half-cocked in the water before me, is to watch my memories being gathered together.

For others it may be a necessary part of the dream, but a fish that has hooked itself is not a part of mine. I need to be the catalyst – the one to set the hook. For some reason I cannot leave the deciding moment on whether or not there's a bend in the rod to a complicated fiendish device on the lake bed that does it all for me. These play no part in my dreams; for me it is my float.

For some, who spin for their fish, the thump on their rod tips will be the moment they long for. Although I'm not a great follower of this method, I will readily admit to having prayed for a take as I spent all those mornings at the lake in Auronzo, patiently and endlessly casting that Mepps. Perhaps the one take I had was enough to fulfil the dream, but until I feel the need to spend every waking moment thinking of that abrupt jolt on my rod tip, the trout out there can feel safe. Then again, a huge perch would be enough to set it all off again. All I need is a glimpse of an unobtainable, monstrous fish cruising through the weeds and my desire to spin would perhaps be burning again.

Or the mere dimple at a tiny dry fly, or the first twitch of line through the surface film, or a delicate take on a free-lined lobworm. All these moments, much as each of them are longed for in their own way, can never be as intoxicating to me as my little porcupine quill and the ripples spreading out from it.

My Finest Hour

I LIFTED MY head and peered over into the next bay. In the shadowy stillness beneath a canopy of ancient willows, I noticed a tiny disturbance edging along the surface amongst a thin carpet of fluffy white willow seeds.

Thinking it was the tip of the back of a large carp, I watched, hoping it would head my way where I was already planning on ambushing it with a small piece of floating flake for its breakfast.

Away from my secluded little scene and out from under the cool reflected shadows of the trees, the morning was promising to be hot and sunny. Blackcaps and whitethroats were calling and the lake was waking up, although the pair of turtle doves seemed to be missing that year.

Scotty and Steve were already into the beginning of their second day's fishing after a full day and night facing each other on opposite sides of the lake. Suppressing any ideas of over-exerting themselves, they'd been happy to spend the previous twenty-four hours watching their lines arrow out into the distance and listening to a cuckoo call all night long.

I'd decided to break the monotony for an hour or two with a loaf of bread and my lovely split cane, Chapman Mk IV. As I passed Steve on my way round to the bay he informed me that Scotty's boredom had been relieved for a few seconds earlier that morning, when a carp he was reeling in fell off.

Piiiiip … piiiiip … piiiiip … my attention returned to the little disturbance in the water which had turned and was now heading directly my way. As I squeezed a small piece of flake around my hook in preparation to cast to it, I heard another piiiiip … piiiiip … piiiiip … and realised that this was no carp but rather the most ridiculously small moorhen chick I'd ever seen – probably not long out of its egg. Not only that, but I'm convinced it thought I was its mother. After great effort, it finally clambered on top of a small lily pad in the water right at my feet and there it sat, looking directly into my eyes, peeping at me. Taking my camera, I set the focus on close-up, leaned forward and took a few photos. As I straightened up, I realised I'd set the focus too close and missed the opportunity of taking the shot of a lifetime.

While concentrating on the little chick through the viewfinder I hadn't noticed a huge common carp which had drifted along the bank and had rested up directly beneath the lily pad, not two feet from the camera lens. Had I zoomed out at that moment I would have had an incredible shot – the pair of them perfectly in frame, with the moorhen chick sitting on the carp's back. Gathering my rod I felt a tinge of guilt as I backed off along the bank, leaving my bewildered little moorhen chick alone on his lily pad, calling for me.

Turning back to another little bay behind me, I knelt behind a stand of yellow flags, and while a couple of uninterested commons cruised back and forth through the lilies at my feet, another drifted out into open water and casually swirled at the odd morsel trapped in the surface film.

Opening the bail arm of my trusty Mitchell 300, I gently flicked out a large piece of fluffy white flake. I knew it would sink at some point, but for a couple of minutes it would float, hopefully intersecting the path of the carp when it returned. For a little while the carp concerned itself with whatever took its fancy, then at precisely the same time it decided to retrace its outward path, the flake began to sink. Unhurriedly it made its way over and sipped it in before it had fallen six inches.

The MkIV took on a slow curve as the carp turned and bore down to the lake bed. The deep water gave me enough time to gather my net and move into a better position behind the reeds. Most of the time the bend of the cane stopped the carp from heading out into the clear water of the bay, but on an increasingly short line there wasn't too much I could do as the fish, a lovely short, deep, common of a little under sixteen pounds, sewed together several lily stems. With some gentle coaxing though, I persuaded it my way and as I drew it over my cane teardrop net, the lily pads rose back in place to the surface.

Releasing the fish, I peered over into the adjacent bay and was pleased to see my little moorhen chick was happily back with its mother.

Quietly moving round to the opposite corner of the bay, I noticed a few carp idly cruising – the tips of their backs lazily breaking the surface. While I made my way down onto the gravel beneath a large overhanging willow I kept my eyes fixed on the nearest fish while folding a small piece of flake around my hook. If, in that instant, I hadn't momentarily dropped my gaze, I wouldn't have seen it – right at my feet and no further from the bank than the width of this page – a huge common carp. It was picking at morsels from amongst a ledge of feathery willow roots, not six inches below the surface. All I needed to do was drop the flake above its head. The carp was aware of the flake the moment it broke through the surface film, and as it gently swayed down, took it as naturally as if it had been a water beetle.

The moment I struck my hook flew straight into the willow tree above my head. Incredibly the carp hadn't noticed anything amiss and carried on picking amongst the roots. As quietly as I could I pulled my hook free, rebaited, and once again dropped the tiny piece of flake into almost no water at all. This time I allowed myself a full second, struck gently and the carp surged off through the lilies into the clear water of the bay. It was already heading down the lake as I struggled to my feet, and as I stood on

M J PLEDGER

the edge of the bank, leaning as far out as I could in an effort to persuade it away from an overhanging bush twenty yards to my right, I happened to glance down in the water directly below me. Unbelievably there was another, almost identical carp that had made its way along the bank, and in a surreal re-enactment, began to feed amongst the feathery roots.

For a good few minutes it continued to feed – totally oblivious to me standing directly above it, playing its brother. Eventually it drifted off through the lilies, leaving me thinking I might actually land the one on my line. I have no doubt whatsoever that had Vince been standing beside me uttering his infamous words of the fish being virtually in the bag, it would have fallen off.

Especially when I drew it over my waiting net. I had the carp lying fully across the net which I had resting on some lily pads but unfortunately a long, thin, twig had jammed across it and it was preventing me from folding the fish into the mesh. Not surprisingly the carp, tired of all this nonsense, rolled off the net and before heading back off into the bay decided to visit an overhanging bush close to the bank. I called over to Steve, and three or four minutes later he came round to help me. Eventually, with his assistance, we guided the fish safely into the net – a stunning common carp an ounce over twenty-five pounds. A few minutes after we watched it glide off through the lilies, Scotty arrived – he'd packed-up and had come round to say goodbye before heading off home.

As we chatted, I hooked up another piece of flake and flicked it out a few yards in front of us to where several carp were cruising in from open water. They veered off to our right, circled round and returned a few minutes later to mop up the free offerings I'd scattered a little earlier. I ignored them though as I was already half-way through playing a gorgeous common carp of fourteen pounds which had bow-waved out from beneath the willow and taken my flake head-on within seconds of it landing.

After returning the fish, I sent out a larger piece of floating crust. Away from the lazy breeze in open water the crust landed perfectly into a calm area of mid-green reflected leaves. As my attention was distracted by the odd cruising fish, many yards away I noticed the deliciously slow materialisation of the underside of a large carp rising like a ghost, vertically beneath my bait. As I watched the great pectorals fan round I never doubted its intentions. From the huge boiling swirl, my gaze dropped to the motionless line off my rod tip.

'Strike. It's gone.' Scotty called as I stood frozen.

I looked back to a second massive swirl, and although in that one fleeting moment I was convinced the crust hadn't been taken cleanly, I couldn't see it in the vortex of water. My line hadn't moved but trusting Scotty's judgement I swept up the rod anyway. Fully expecting to strike into nothing I was pleasantly surprised to find the cane curling round, following a massive bow wave out into the open water of the bay. Time and time again I countered the fish's every move and soon guided it through the lily pads to Steve and the waiting net.

A glorious linear mirror carp of 18 lb 4 oz – it was truly a fitting end to a perfect hour's fishing.

To Rise a Fish

I REMEMBER CLEARLY the very first time I cast a fly. It was 1978, shortly after Pietra and I got married. A lovely warm summer's evening, there I stood on one of the wooden stages at Netherhall Trout Fishery in Nazeing looking out across the lake. Feeling ridiculously outgunned without my Mitchell 308 and lobworms, I looked dolefully at the flyrod in my hand and, even more mournfully, at the miserable tuft of feathers hanging on the line in the other.

I'd been watching a few of the other flyfishers and I suppose at some point I decided all I needed to do was pull enough line off the reel, wave the rod around a bit and aim it at the lake. My very first series of waves sent a whole snarl of line lakewards and then, after about twelve feet or so, gravity,

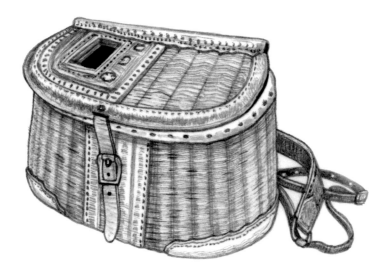

deciding enough was enough, dumped the whole lot straight into the water at my feet. I will say in my defence that the coils of fly line as they came splashing down fell in almost concentric circles with the leader following behind and the fly, such as it was, finally spiralling down smack in the middle of the big tangled heap like a shot-down plane. While I was winding the lot in a trout came up, and within the great coot's nest of flyline, took the fly and swam off with it. Surprised as we both were, a few minutes later the trout and I were saying hello, eye to eye, on the bank. Quite what we were both thinking of each other as I gently removed the hook and released it, I really can't imagine.

In the intervening years I've honed whatever casting abilities I may have been born with and on my best day I might just be able to convince a few fish that my fly is worth looking at. That is when it's not hanging from a branch.

Not too long ago there was a knock at the door and a parcel from America I'd been eagerly awaiting finally arrived. A Geiger antique wicker creel that I just had to take to see the stream. So I gathered my wand-like 6 ft brook rod and minute fly reel loaded with a weight-forward 2 wt floating line, a few dry flies and a tiny 1930s ash and cane teardrop landing net, and headed off along the meandering River Stort just between Hoddesdon and Harlow. It was a warm sunny afternoon, with all the colours mixed for a perfect hour or two fishing. I think I was the first person to walk the banks for months as all the waterside vegetation, the spring growth, was waist high and undisturbed.

Sand martins had already arrived and I could hear a cuckoo in the distance as kingfishers flew around checking out the stream. Damselflies lifted out from the bankside reeds as I quietly pushed my way through, just downstream of a sweeping bend. As I emerged through the reeds, I crouched on the gravel at the water's edge. I was on the inside of a bend as it swept round towards me, the rippling water at my feet only two inches deep where the current's pace quickened, racing through the narrowest of gullies behind me. Quite literally, if I took one step to my right, then another, I'd be pulling myself up through the reeds on the opposite bank. I had to keep a wary eye on a steep gravel bank behind me as I suspected there might be an old kingfisher's nest just below the overhanging grass along the ridge. Had I seen a kingfisher come along to inspect it I would have moved upstream, but as they were calling a few bends below me, I was happy that I wasn't disturbing them.

I turned my attention to the water upstream where it creased the base of another vertical bank about three feet high and noticed an almost indiscernible rise about six inches from the edge. I'd seen a few minnows and dace flip about ten yards upstream where the bend began to sweep round – tiny fish wildly snipping at the odd insect in the current. The rise which interested me was probably only fifteen feet in front of where I was standing and I could have almost stretched over and touched the decreasing ripples with my rod tip. As I watched, a dark shape again rose in the current and gently took another struggling insect. With these two rises

it became obvious the breeze was dislodging insects, probably tiny beetles, from the tufts of grass overhanging the vertical bank. As they dropped into the water, fish were simply holding tight in the current, waiting for them to drift down. The fish were aware of the insects drifting towards them before I was, as every time I noticed a dark shape begin to rise from the streambed, it was clear that another one was heading their way.

After the insect was taken it took an instant for the fish to melt back into the slightly deeper water. I'm guessing that the point where they were holding up was at most sixteen inches deep, but because of my colour blindness, once they'd drifted down a few inches, they were lost to me against the browny-green background.

Choosing a fly was simple enough – anything small that floated.

Using a short tapered leader of about six feet, I only needed one pull off the reel to drop the fly slightly upstream of where the fish were holding. After a drift towards me of a couple of feet, the shape which rose from the bottom to meet my fly had me breathless. Time after time this happened and very few casts failed to move a fish, although quite a few times I missed on the strike. Several times after I'd missed, I simply kept the fly in the air and brought it back down in front of them again.

In the space of about forty-five minutes I landed nine chub of between three and five pounds, and the only water I had to play them out was where they were holed up. Incredibly they were not disturbed, even with me crunching around on the gravel and taking photos of them alongside my new antique creel before I released them. Quite simply, had I not noticed that first delicate rise, I would not have known there was anything there, least of all a large shoal of big chub.

Magical Crucians

LOOKING AT A magical little crucian carp painting by Ernest Petts my heart is ten years old again and in my mind's eye I see my float, a large red-tipped cork affair, out in the water in front of me. I am at Barclay Park in Hoddesdon in the 1960s. Then I was sure there was nowhere on earth where a float looked better – cocked maybe a foot from the lilies if I was lucky enough to get it that close. Two feet below the float was a little round pellet of chewed bread and the only thing to suggest magic was about to happen was a ripple or two circling out from it. Mostly that was as near as I got and it was only when I replaced my big float with a tiny porcupine quill that the little crucians began to pay me more regular visits. I marvelled at how the delicate three- and four-inch long fish curled in my hand as I gently released them, watching them skitter back to their friends by the lilies.

Later, during the summers of 1970 and 1971, Vince, Chad and I fished for them – our favourite swim was inside the curve of the large lily patch we named the Horseshoe. Somehow we'd all cram our floats inside the curve and many days and nights were spent catching lovely crucians to just over a pound.

On one memorable day, with Chad sitting in the middle, our floats either side of his, a few feet apart, Vince and I had simultaneous bites. So Chad reeled in his line to give both of us a little more space in which to play our fish out. And it was quite a fight. When Vince's fish zigged, mine zagged. When his zagged, mine zigged. Zig-zagging around the swim, they gradually met in the middle and as we brought them to the net, we found we were playing the same fish – a crucian of 14 oz with a hook in either side of its mouth.

This fish belies the usually cautious nature of crucian carp. Throughout the 1970s and 1980s, Vince, Chad, Scotty and I spent countless days and evenings fishing for these little carp at Taylor's Lake, one of our club lakes at Pig Lane in Bishop's Stortford. A natural lake nestling alongside the

148

River Stort, Taylor's is truly delightful, in that even if you spent fifteen minutes walking all the way round it, you would always find another swim more beautiful than the one you'd chosen. It is a maze of secluded corners, bays and islands, where overhanging alders and weeping willows cast leafy shadows over lazy beds of lilies. For a few seasons even that rare plant, the Water Soldier, could be found, floating to the surface to flower. Monet and Tunnicliffe would have found peace there, with much to paint amongst the darting dragonflies. No doubt Monet would have been looking beyond Tunnicliffe's clucking moorhens, preferring to concentrate on light flickering across lily petals as they reflected haloes among dappled pads. I can see Tunnicliffe's compositions in every turn of my eye – moorhens with heads dipped, ducking secretly between wobbling pads. It's what happens underneath the surface that feeds my imagination though – a world of little crucians, pirouetting, dancing and truffling among the fronds of Canadian pondweed. As I gaze at my yellow-tipped porcupine quill I know the little fish are gathering below – now and then they brush against my line, causing my heart to beat just that little bit faster.

And now the scene is set. Here they gyrate, twist and turn among vortexes of their own making, completely oblivious to me anchored to my little float in the world above. There I sit, pondering and wondering why my favourite porcupine quill, with the mere tip of yellow breaking the surface, wafting and swaying among a carpet of effervescing bubbles, refuses to do anything which prompts me to strike.

I will not insult such a happy little fish by trying to catch one with anything but the lightest of tackle and, more appropriately, the most natural and traditional I can use. Maybe a boy's rod like the Allcock's Lucky Strike, matched with an Illingworth threadline reel or perhaps Paul Witcher's three-and-a-half inch Longford Aerial – a creation of the gods.

In the early days at Taylor's things were a little easier. Whereas I rarely strayed from my beloved yellow-tipped porcupines, Vince insisted on anything with an infuriating red tip, while Chad usually fished with a long white peacock quill – at least something I could see. Scotty loved his red-tipped Stillwater Blues. Because of my colour blindness I spent no end of time trying to find them against reflected leafy backgrounds, especially in the autumn. Bait was invariably soft bread paste and the crucians behaved like ordinary fish – we caught loads. On hot sunny days after a spell of loose-feeding we even caught them on slow-sinking maggots – while we watched the palm-sized golden flashes twisting and turning in the dark reflections as they rose up in the water in a mad rush to catch the bait.

Recently however, for reasons we never really understood, Taylor's crucians have decided to forget how they used to behave years ago and now we are resigned to sit and watch as our floats rock and sway among a cauldron of bubbles.

I have the impression that they do not even know that we are there. For although they are indeed attracted by the succulent free offerings we trickle in, the way they carry on, seemingly with complete abandon, is at times mildly infuriating. Mildly infuriating because, even with the most delicately presented fine tackle, they have this unnerving knack of brushing it all aside, leaving us staring at a float which may as well have a little smiley face painted on the side which laughs back at us.

But fortunately, very occasionally, something goes wrong in the crucian plan and I find myself holding one of these little fish in my hand. And as I meet the cheeky look in its eye I am reminded of Ernest Petts on a nice sunny afternoon forty years ago, when magic truly flowed from his brush.

Do You Take This Crucian?

SATURDAY, 23 JULY, 1977 – Taylor's Lake. Chad's peacock quill rose slightly, dithered a while, dipped maybe a few times, went off on a little run, came back and almost lay flat, but didn't. I would have struck six or seven times by then and almost certainly I would have missed – just as Chad did when it finally went flying under.

We were sitting side-by-side in our favourite swim on the causeway, our quills resting at opposite sides of a patch we'd raked just off the bank of amphibious bistort. The dawn mist was wafted around on the surface by an idle breeze, and shards of sunlight were flicking across the water, illuminating little diamonds of light amongst the bubbles effervescing around the floats. Crucians were truffling in the groundbait and enjoying the breakfast table we'd laid out for them. Time and again we re-enacted the same scene and as the morning wore on the crucians lost their usual caution and we began catching a few.

I turned to Chad as he was bringing yet another to the net:

'What time have we got to pack up?'

'As long as I'm home by two, it'll be okay.'

Chad was going to be best man at our friend Martyn Rice's wedding that afternoon. Ahead of us we had a twenty minute drive back to Hoddesdon where he'd have to drop me off, then head off home to Ware, get severely cleaned up and then drive back out again to the wedding.

The crucians fed and fed and we caught and caught – lovely fish up to just over a pound. It was fast becoming one of those memorable days when, no matter what we did, we caught fish. Except now, as we slipped the last crucian into the net, we were out of hook bait.

Time was running out and with our impending pack-up time looming ever nearer, Chad had to resort to moulding the last of the groundbait into pliable balls from which we could eke out a few more casts. If anything the crucians appreciated this new bait even more and within seconds of it reaching bottom, they were on it – some even took it on the drop. I could sense that Chad, with that calculating mathematical brain of his was working out every conceivable second we had left, and at what last cliff-edge moment we'd need to pack up. We added a few 'last cast' crucians to the equation, weighed and photographed the catch, packed up doubly, triply, quick and hurried off to his faithful old Morris Minor.

Loading it up even more quickly we sped off, confident in his maths, heading for Hoddesdon. My gaze drifted to the dashboard and I saw that the 'E' on the fuel gauge was hidden behind the indicator needle.

'Er, Chad, I think you'll have to fill it up mate, we're not going to get back.'

As we approached a garage, I could see him looking at the price display at the entrance as we sailed past.

'That's 2p dearer than in Ware. I'm not paying that.'

'You'll only need a gallon mate, I really think you'd better put some in.'

We sped past the next garage and the next, and as we approached open countryside, I began to have serious doubts the car would reach anywhere, let alone a wedding. Then at the point where the countryside couldn't get more open, the engine began to labour and the indicator needle on the speedometer began to flicker and descend to join its neighbour on the fuel gauge. I will admit it did lift momentarily a couple of times during the last two hundred yards before it finally gave up, and as the old Morris ground to a halt the indicator fell lifeless on the nought.

Running out of petrol had obviously not been a consideration in Chad's computations of how many last gasp crucians could conceivably be squeezed into a successful, trouble-free, trip to Hoddesdon. And as lovely as the day was, with skylarks singing gaily over open fields and blue tits pecking among the hedgerow blossoms, and flights of pigeons flying over the absolutely immobile Morris Minor, Chad began to rue the occasions he sped by the petrol pumps.

Stranded a mile from Stanstead Abbotts, I ran down the hill into town

M.J.PLEDGER.

to find a telephone box. After trying a few numbers, I finally tracked down Vince who was busy at home, lounging on a settee scratching his ear. As I dragged my way back up the hill, I found Chad doing his best trying to make time stand still by pulling his hair out and talking to the skylarks.

After an age, Vince eventually arrived with a container of petrol – he had to try several garages before one would agree to sell him some without him needing to fill up his own car. Life was breathed back into the old Morris, the engine fired up, dials flickered and we continued on our way.

To this day I have no idea how on earth Chad managed to make it to the wedding in time, but he did. Just think – we could have had a few more minutes with the crucians.

Things That Go Bump ...

It was years ago but I remember the scream well ...

I was night fishing at Shell Lake, Hatfield Forest. The glow from my hurricane lamp was friendly and warm and the beam from my Pifco lantern skimmed out across the water illuminating my peacock quill. Leaning back in my chair, arms folded and head to one side, I was idly listening to snippets of conversation between a dad and his young son drifting through the darkness a couple of swims to my right.

Tiredness overcoming the young boy, he told his dad he was heading back to the car for a sleep, and that he was leaving his dad a half-eaten Mars bar on the ground beside his chair for him in case he got hungry later.

The following morning I ambled along the bank and asked the guy what on earth the banshee-like scream was that echoed around the lake during the night. Apparently, five minutes after his son had left he remembered the Mars bar on the ground and leant over to pick it up. Unfortunately, a large rat had just beaten him to it, which was a shame really, because grabbing it across the back probably shortened his own life by a couple of weeks.

The nature of darkness being what it is, that is *dark* – it allows small, undesirable things to happen to us which would not be the case in daylight. Like idly picking up half a cup of coffee I'd forgotten about, putting it to my lips and finding a massive great leopard slug curled up inside it.

Sometimes though the surprises happen to other people, which then become amusing rather than scary.

It was around 11.30 p.m. and I was happily sitting on the towpath a few hundred yards up from Rye House tavern on the River Lea. Behind me was a bright security light which lit up my immediate area, allowing me to watch my float without need for a torch. A lovely summer's evening, nice and warm, I was contentedly sitting in my little halo of light surrounded by darkness on all sides. People began leaving the tavern and as I continued to miss a few bites on my peacock quill, two young couples passed behind me on their way home. Just before they disappeared into the night, I hit a bite and began playing what turned out to be an extremely irate eel of about two pounds. Looking over his shoulder, while the others carried on, one of the guys walked back to see what I was struggling with.

'What's that?' he asked.

'An eel.' I said

'Is it poisonous?'

'No.'

'Does it sting?'

'No.'

So he asked me if he could take it to show his girlfriend, who was by now down the towpath somewhere in the darkness, oblivious to what was going on in the head of her brainless companion.

I'll admit to being quite surprised at how he managed to stay attached to the eel, as he hurried along the bank to show it to his girlfriend. I wasn't that convinced though that it was going to impress her much. There was a full ten seconds of delicious silence before the inevitable blood-curdling scream, followed by a loud echoing splash as the eel finally made its way back home.

Because I'd had a decidedly unpleasant encounter with a ghost when I was in bed one night decades before when I was eleven, you could say I had an open mind regarding the existence of such things.

Proof of this starts with the simple act of me taking an unwanted white wooden gate along to our lake at Nazeing to be used by our working party that was busy shoring up a swim known as Leathers. The gate was perfect, we wedged it under the bank and then buried it under a load of hardcore and gravel.

Then one autumn evening, months later, I decided to set up in the Gate Swim, about 20 yards to the right of Leathers. I was the only person fishing on either of the two lakes that night and probably because of this a feeling of slight uneasiness started creeping in. As I sat behind my rods the evening began to pull in and with the encroaching darkness my unease increased.

As I kept looking at my watch, my attention was drawn to every little creak and rustle in the bushes. There was also an unearthly calm to the evening which made things worse. Then as it got darker I began to be aware of an eerie white glow, almost human in shape, standing about twenty yards to my left along the bank. The narrow path and the tunnel of trimmed hawthorns heightening the awful vision of what was standing there, watching me, watching it. Pulling my umbrella lower had neither the desired effect of making me feel easier – or protecting me from whatever I thought was out there. Forty-five minutes of this had me literally too scared to move. It started to rain – one of those autumn drizzles, and as I sat there frozen in my chair, praying for neither of my indicators to move, my left-hander crept up to the butt.

It had to be struck and I cursed my luck as my rod hooped over. Moving as little as possible I played it out, netted it and lay it on some grass. By now my nerves were shot to pieces and all I wanted was not be there.

It was a wild carp of about five pounds. I lit my small torch and as the glow moved across its face, every conceivable nerve which was holding me together, fell apart.

The fish had no eye.

At the precise moment when I least needed anything to tip me over the edge, that was it. The fish had been born without a right eye. Where it should have been was as smooth as its gill plate. I slipped it back and hunched over again, not daring to move a muscle. Then, for no explicable reason other than the thought that I might as well get things over with, I straightened up and calmly walked over to the deathly white apparition which was still standing there watching me. Drawn to whatever fate it had in store for me.

As I approached, it became brighter and brighter as if from another dimension … the white wooden gate which some idiot had dug up and left leaning against a tree.

At that point, even with the realisation that I wasn't going to be vaporised by a death ray, I packed everything away, got back to the safety of my car and drove off. It was now 2 a.m. Driving down the dark lane with all the surreal events behind me, I approached a T-junction and stopped. As I paused to look down to change gear and move off, my eyes lifted to the awful vision of a dishevelled old tramp clambering out of a reedy ditch which he'd obviously fallen into and metamorphosing, zombie-like, in front of me. Half-an-hour later, curled up safely in bed I lay awake the rest of the night waiting for it to get light.

One night on the same lake my good friend, Bob Jermy, was also testament to being on the wrong end of what the darkness had to offer. He was stretched out on his bed chair, no doubt enjoying the warmth and comfort of drifting off into a deep sleep, when Albert, the slinky grey cat who lived at the lake, leapt, claws-extended, onto his stomach.

Quietly studying Bob on the odd occasion over the years, I often wonder whether he completely got over it

Night Fishing

THE EXPECTANCY WITH which we wait as darkness approaches must surely be one of our greatest pleasures. No matter where or how we fish, that same delicious anticipation is the same for us all.

I find there is something undeniably childlike in the feeling I get when I fish through the hours of darkness. The feeling of actually being old enough to be allowed to go fishing at night – the feeling of uncertainty, of fear almost – of being awake during the hours when everyone else is sleeping. These feelings I most certainly had when I started to fish at night when I was fourteen, and they have never left me. Better still to share these stolen hours with close friends, and frequently it's these memories which remain the keenest.

The early 1970s were such times when Vince, Chad and I fished through the night hoping for tench and bream at the North Met Pit in Cheshunt. Often on the same evenings, Steve would be fishing about a hundred yards along in the darkness to our right with his mate Alan Himbry. One of our favourite spots was on a short section of bank just to the left of an expansive reed bed. Steve and Alan would invariably fish from the end of a long spit of land which ranged far out into the bay overlooking the other end of the reeds.

Although we all arrived and set up during the afternoon, usually on a Saturday, nothing really happened until long after dark. We all float fished bunches of maggots or bread flake a couple of rod lengths out, in eight to ten feet of water. As darkness began to close in, our limit of vision receded until we lit up the water in front of us with large torches. Three beams skimmed across the surface, lighting up long white peacock quills fixed bottom end only, and there each of us sat in anticipation of what might happen.

As was our custom in those days, and because of the expense of the large square torch batteries, we'd squeeze out the remaining glow from the previous trip's battery until it finally gave up, usually around midnight, and then change it over for a new one. I remember well the first fishing torch Dad bought me – a Pifco red dome battery lantern. The fits of giggles and laughter soon began to wear off as inevitably tiredness befell us. Heavy lidded, our three figures would become progressively more hunched in our fishing chairs, until at some point during the night we'd each drift off into a fitful sleep. Waking up we'd take some comfort in the friendly glow and warmth of our hurricane lamps before drifting off again.

In the periphery of semi-consciousness I'd notice both Vince and Chad still slumped in their chairs, and reaching down for my hurricane lamp would quietly pick it up and cradle it on my knees. Checking that the floats

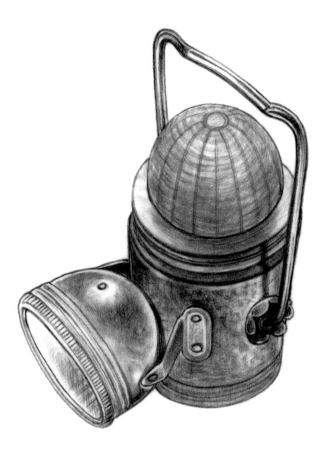

hadn't moved, I would allow myself to drop back a couple of notches towards sleep and through half-closed eyes gaze into the lamp. I was custodian of the floats while the others slept but the intimacy and warmth of the lamp would draw me in.

I would find myself quietly amused by tiny mosquitoes and sedges as they flew in from the darkness attracted by the glow and watched as they bumbled drunkenly around on the glass. The almost intoxicating smell of burning paraffin and the low hiss of the lamp held what was still awake of me in a hypnotic state. Even at that point of low-consciousness I would be aware of a number of tiny things. Like a few gnats which had accidentally flown inside the glass and were contorting crazily in the heat, or a stripy black-and-yellow snail that had finally made it to the top of my flask, having started its journey when I was asleep.

Either I would wake Vince and Chad or the sedge warbler would. Normally the warblers would sing all night. Perhaps it was the incessant warbling which sent the other two to sleep or perhaps it was what half woke me up. In that state of almost-sleep, thoughts and reasoning become as irrational as dreams.

Tench could turn up at any hour but the bream usually showed after 2 a.m., by which time we were all pretty much half-asleep. The characteristic lazy lifting, tilting and slide-away bites would generate a big enough burst of adrenaline to temporarily allow us to land a couple of fish. In the main we'd only catch a bream or two each trip, but they were large fish up to 7 lb or more. A further touch of magic was added one night when Chad caught a glorious crucian carp of 2 lb 4 oz. It may have been on the very same night that Steve also caught a crucian weighing an incredible 3 lb 1 oz.

Wonderful times, and mixed with incidents of childish pranks, the North Met night trips remain treasured memories for all of us. But perhaps slightly less treasured in Chad's case if he looks back at a particular occasion when Vince and I saved and prepared a swim for him directly on top of a wasp's nest. Then later during the night after he and the wasps fell asleep, we carefully arranged his hissing hurricane lamp right under his backside.

A nice touch we thought.

Last Casts

INEVITABLY THE TIME of the last cast draws near, and unwelcome as it is, on very rare occasions it may come with a little surprise. I don't mean our first last cast, nor even the second or third, as we all have a few of these tucked in our back pocket, but the *real absolutely final* last cast. Ever mindful a straggler could be ambling through and ever hopeful our bait might just tempt him into having a last minute snack before he disappears off into the reeds. Most of the time our idle thoughts count for nothing and we reel in. Most of the time …

It was around October in 1971 – Steve and I were finishing off the day towards the end of Barbara's stretch at King's Weir, waiting for Dad to arrive. It was a long walk from Slipe Lane to where we were but he enjoyed it nonetheless and always found things to photograph on the way down. My eyes start to well up as I remember him approaching along the bank, camera round his neck, in his old familiar green jacket and woolly bobble hat that Mum had knitted for him.

'No rush, fish on for a bit.'

As far as I knew Dad had never held a rod in his life, so as I cleared away a few bits and pieces I handed him mine,

'Here, you have a go.'

I'd been trotting all day without much to show for it and the old peacock quill was already set about three feet deep. Two or three minutes to show him how to open the bail arm on the 308, an underhand flick and two maggots were trundling down the stream maybe perhaps twelve feet out. If I hadn't turned round to sort something out in my bag I swear I would have seen Pixie Dust falling all around him.

'The float's gone.'

'What?'

'The float's gone.'

I turned and there he was, laughing his head off as he reeled in. By the

time I got to him the fish was swinging on two feet of line from the rod tip waiting for me to sort it out.

One of the rarest of captures – a tiny barbel of maybe four inches. I took a couple of photos of Dad holding it before he released it back to the water to find his little mates. Only one other time in my life have I seen a barbel to match it – one I caught myself, along with an unbelievable minnow of four inches and a seven-and-a-half inch gudgeon from the tiny weir pool above King's Weir. Truly the sixpence jar moment to cap them all.

Another of my real last casts, again involving Dad, was during our cheese puff era at Nazeing. Dad had joined me for the afternoon and as we sat side-by-side in the Telegraph swim on the big pit a small number of carp were happily swirling around the cheese puffs we'd catapulted out. For some reason it was one of those days when every one of my strikes amounted to nothing. Dad sat looking through the binoculars, getting more and more exasperated every time I missed yet another completely unmissable take. The ducks and seagulls were also driving us both insane and I think they probably took more cheese puffs than the carp did. In amongst all these fevered activities one carp in particular stood out. He had a high humpy back and was considerably larger than the shoal of wildies he was hanging around with, and every now and then he would serenely suck in the cheese puff that had my hook in it. Each time I looked at Dad in complete amazement as I wound in yet again after another fruitless strike.

'Right, that's it, I've had enough. He can stay out there.'

Dad turned to me with that look of his.

'Stick it out again.'

'Okay, this really is the last one, that thing's driving me nuts.'

For a full five minutes the cheese puff sat in the lake about forty yards out. A couple of mallards had seen it and were heading in from several yards away. Resigned to one of them eating it, I waited until the very last moment to strike it off the hook, and at precisely the same time there was a massive swirl and my rod tip crawled over. By the time the two mallards had worked out that their last party snack was now heading towards Dad with the landing net, the carp was ours. A truly immaculate mirror carp, almost a leather, and weighing 15 lb 4 oz.

I must leave Vince to have the last word on last casts though.

Not long ago we'd decided to finish off the very last day of the season in our favourite swim, the Beach, King's Weir. As can easily be the way of things at the Beach, the chub sometimes seem to want to stay in bed all day and no amount of bouncing lobworms on top of them will wake them up. Something I personally find hard to come to terms with but there you go, I'm not a chub.

Vince had spent the day as he usually does, just a couple of feet to the left of me, messing around with all kinds of baits, rigs and things foreign to me. With perhaps an hour left of daylight, he took his rod and chair and disappeared into Swim No. 2 just to my right. More fiddling with ridiculous things like hair-rigs, pellets and who knows what else, followed by a splash out in front of him under some trailing branches. Apparently the splash was a big pellet on a hair rig, finished off with one of my giant lobworms on the hook, just in case.

A few hours later it had got dark and it was pretty obvious to me every chub in the river was elsewhere.

'Vince, I think I'm packing up mate.'

'Yeah, I suppose you're right.'

So, on the last day of the season, on his last cast, on the very last second, he leaned forward to pick up his rod. As his hand gripped the corks, the tip flew round, and he was, instead of reeling in, playing a fish.

I grabbed the net and rushed over to where he was playing a very big chub indeed. In the reflection of the lights from Barbara's windows in the lock house, Vince drew the chub over my waiting net.

An impossibly huge chub – the needle on the scales finally gave up at 7 lb 8 oz.

Truly, one of the monsters of the pool.

And so as you all return to your swim and float, I'll return to mine.

I had my last cast a while ago, but when I reeled in, the bait was still okay, so I thought there'd be no harm in putting it out again. The light is dropping, the lily pads are moving and a few bubbles are rising up to the surface. You'll have to excuse me as you close the covers, I think I'll continue to sit a while …

… Oh well then, just one more.

AND FINALLY

The real absolutely final last cast

Auronzo Di Cadore[*]

QUANDO RITORNO, VOGLIO essere un gran orso. (When I return I want to be a big bear). These were Uncle Sergio's words when I asked him what he wanted to be after he died. I asked him why a bear?

'I'd live up in the mountains where no one would bother me. Half the year I'd sleep through all the bad weather, and in the summer I'd do nothing but fish all day, and eat fruit and berries.'

Because Dad loved foxes, I said I'd like to return as a fox, and as all this silliness seemed a million years away, we fell over each other laughing and laughing.

Many years later and facing what to us was the far too early inevitability of such things, my Aunty Laura and I returned to the old cemetery by the canal on the outskirts of Bologna where I'd once seen the giant peacock moth as a child and where Uncle Sergio was now at rest.

It was one of the hardest things I've ever had to do, and weighed down with grief I stood before Sergio's resting place, his photo on the wall signifying where he now lay beside other departed souls. Glancing either side of him, unbelievably, the name of the person on his left was *Volpe* (fox), and the one on his right, *Orsolino* (young bear). At that precise moment I was filled with an overpowering warmth – I was aware he was with me and that he would never leave my side. Just as I know that his spirit wanders

[*] Auronzo di Cadore is situated on the shores of Lake Santa Caterina about 120 km north of Venice, in the province of Belluno in the Dolomites of Northern Italy.)

the mountains he loved, sitting among the wild cyclamen and gentians growing on the slopes of the Dolomites in northern Italy, where our family spent our holidays in my younger years.

Just as the scent of western balsams pervades my fondest memories of Italy, so too the unforgettable times Sergio and I spent collecting and eating tiny succulent wild mountain strawberries from the shady grassy slopes between the pine trees.

One of my fondest and silliest memories was of Sergio and I sitting by the side of a mountain lake. Dad took some slides of the pair of us under a stand of balsams, flicking tiny pieces of bread from our paninis to a little shoal of minute fry which shimmered in the surface film at our feet. Every time they swam too close we'd whack the water with little sticks sending them off in blind panic, only for them to return a minute later for another go.

Then there's another memory – nothing to do with fishing but of being strapped in an open single chair lift, halfway up the side of a mountain with the brand-new windcheater Mum had bought me over my lap. As I looked down past my dangling legs with the tops of the poplars passing far beneath, Mum, in the seat in front, turned to me and said:

'Whatever you do, don't drop your jacket.'

I think I managed to say half of 'as if I would', before it spiralled down and down amongst a patchwork of trees. Trying to make a mental note of where it fell was just about as pointless as Mum telling me not to drop it in the first place. When we reached the top of the mountain, Sergio and I climbed down the mountain slope and followed the line of the chair lift above us, in the vain hope of finding it.

Several times we retraced our path back up towards the summit after I told him I recognised a particular tree but in the end after several hours of laughing, clambering and falling over rocks, we gave up and returned to the base of the chair lift where we'd started out. I'll never forget Mum standing there, holding the bloody thing up, after some climbers had handed it in not long after I'd dropped it.

I remember too, another holiday we had in the Dolomites, in early August, 1970. I was fifteen and as smitten by fishing as anyone had the right to be. On this occasion we were staying in Auronzo di Cadore and if the passage of time had any scrap of decency it would have left us all there. The moment we arrived, Sergio and I left the others to do all the necessarily unnecessary things like checking in and unpacking, while we did the important things like check out the routes out of town to the hills and the lake.

It is no wonder this is where Sergio wanted his bear spirit to roam. Waking in the early mornings to the sound of church bells and opening old wooden shutters to alpine choughs wheeling across the mountain slopes. Going down to breakfast and sitting outside at the tables, taking in the scent of freshly-watered geraniums in the window boxes, and breaking off pieces of warm crusty Italian bread to feed the sparrows which came hopping, ever hopeful, between our feet under the chairs.

Best of all, we used to stroll through the town, taking in the smells of the coffee shops and bakeries, then follow one of the many off-shoot roads that wound steeply up into the hills. Often for no reason other than to reach one of the ancient stone drinking fountains where water, fresh from the mountains, would gush ice cold from a tap in the rock.

As usual on holiday, I'd taken my rod and yet another Mitchell that followed me home – a 410. I'd filled the shallow spool with 2 lb Maxima, and although I'd yet to use it, I'd polished it and wound the handle and clicked the bail arm over so much I'd almost worn the gears out.

My rod, which was a 10 ft two-piece hollow glass carp rod, had been made for me by one of my brother Doug's friends in our fishing club. I'd lost count of the number of times I'd varnished it, just because I liked it so much. I used to make up the rod in the hotel and after breakfast rush down to the lake at the edge of town. But not so fast that the passers-by couldn't get a good look of my shiny 410 and even shinier rod. It was quite a long walk over to the other side of the lake, but the long line of poplars there seemed to pull at me.

The first morning I spent a couple of hours idly sitting behind my rod with the line arrowing out to a bait of Great-uncle Fidenzio's magic concoction but, because of my impatience, rather than the lack of smell of the bait (which was never in doubt), I reeled in and cut the line. I tied on a small Mepps No.1 spinner and wandered the bank casting anywhere there might have been a trout. Whether the trout knew it or not, they were never where they should have been. That's if any were there at all.

Mum even came down on a couple of occasions to sit with her weekly Italian puzzle magazine, *Settimana Enigmistica*, and do the crosswords. Not once was there a sign that fish existed in the lake. But on the sixth morning, a morning just like all the others, from alongside a short row of bushes which overhung the bank, the Mepps did its stuff. I must have retrieved it dozens of times along that same spot all the way back to my rod tip, but this time, just this once, the spinner stopped dead, the rod tip pulled around and the lake echoed with the chaotic thumping of a trout that just couldn't pass it up.

I drew the trout to the net, a lovely brownie of exactly two pounds, and admired it like no other trout I've caught since. In between it jumping around on the grass, I took some photos and we said goodbye, closing the book on my trout fishing in the Dolomites.

Nothing more than that – one insignificant trout in the great scheme of things has tied together untold memories that will stay with me until I'll no longer be reeling in. Although I've caught any number of trout since that day, most of which I cannot even begin to remember, that one alone has knitted together so many fond memories of my past, I find there's no real need or even desire to catch another. But then it did have the advantage of being caught on the far side of the lake while I was under the influence of the sweet, sweet, aroma of the western balsam poplars.